AA004143

SIMUL 2018

The Tenth International Conference on Advances in System Simulation

October 14 - 18, 2018

Nice, France

SIMUL 2018 Editors

Arash Ramezani, The Helmut Schmidt University, Germany

Printed from e-media with permission by:

Curran Associates, Inc.
57 Morehouse Lane
Red Hook, NY 12571

Some format issues inherent in the e-media version may also appear in this print version.

Copyright© (2018) by International Academy, Research, and Industry Association (IARIA)
Please refer to the Copyright Information page.

Printed by Curran Associates, Inc. (2018)

International Academy, Research, and Industry Association (IARIA)
412 Derby Way
Wilmington, DE 19810

Phone: (408) 893-6407
Fax: (408) 527-6351

petre@iaria.org

Additional copies of this publication are available from:

Curran Associates, Inc.
57 Morehouse Lane
Red Hook, NY 12571 USA
Phone: 845-758-0400
Fax: 845-758-2633
Email: curran@proceedings.com
Web: www.proceedings.com

Table of Contents

SIMUL 2018

Forward

The Tenth International Conference on Advances in System Simulation (SIMUL 2018), held on October 14 - 18, 2018- Nice, France, continued a series of events focusing on advances in simulation techniques and systems providing new simulation capabilities.

While different simulation events are already scheduled for years, SIMUL 2018 identified specific needs for ontology of models, mechanisms, and methodologies in order to make easy an appropriate tool selection. With the advent of Web Services and WEB 3.0 social simulation and human-in simulations bring new challenging situations along with more classical process simulations and distributed and parallel simulations. An update on the simulation tool considering these new simulation flavors was aimed at, too.

The conference provided a forum where researchers were able to present recent research results and new research problems and directions related to them. The conference sought contributions to stress-out large challenges in scale system simulation and advanced mechanisms and methodologies to deal with them. The accepted papers covered topics on social simulation, transport simulation, simulation tools and platforms, simulation methodologies and models, and distributed simulation.

We welcomed technical papers presenting research and practical results, position papers addressing the pros and cons of specific proposals, such as those being discussed in the standard forums or in industry consortiums, survey papers addressing the key problems and solutions on any of the above topics, short papers on work in progress, and panel proposals.

We take here the opportunity to warmly thank all the members of the SIMUL 2018 technical program committee as well as the numerous reviewers. The creation of such a broad and high quality conference program would not have been possible without their involvement. We also kindly thank all the authors that dedicated much of their time and efforts to contribute to the SIMUL 2018. We truly believe that thanks to all these efforts, the final conference program consists of top quality contributions.

This event could also not have been a reality without the support of many individuals, organizations and sponsors. We also gratefully thank the members of the SIMUL 2018 organizing committee for their help in handling the logistics and for their work that is making this professional meeting a success. We gratefully appreciate to the technical program committee co-chairs that contributed to identify the appropriate groups to submit contributions.

We hope the SIMUL 2018 was a successful international forum for the exchange of ideas and results between academia and industry and to promote further progress in simulation research. We also hope Nice provided a pleasant environment during the conference and everyone saved some time for exploring this beautiful city.

SIMUL 2018 Steering Committee

Hendrik Rothe, Helmut-Schmidt-Universität/ Universität der Bundeswehr Hamburg, Germany
Witold Pedrycz, University of Alberta, Canada
Ian Flood, University of Florida, USA

Marek Bauer, Politechnika Krakowska, Poland
Mu-Chun Su, National Central University, Taiwan
Etienne Kerre, Ghent University, Belgium
Kuan Yew Wong, Universiti Teknologi Malaysia (UTM), Malaysia
Yao Yiping, National University of Defence Technology - Changsha, Hunan, P. R. China

SIMUL 2018 Industry/Research Advisory Committee

Tsan-sheng Hsu, Institute of Information Science | Academia Sinica, Taiwan
Letizia Nicoletti, Cal-tek srl, Italy

SIMUL 2018

Committee

SIMUL Steering Committee

Hendrik Rothe, Helmut-Schmidt-Universität/ Universität der Bundeswehr Hamburg, Germany
Witold Pedrycz, University of Alberta, Canada
Ian Flood, University of Florida, USA
Marek Bauer, Politechnika Krakowska, Poland
Mu-Chun Su, National Central University, Taiwan
Etienne Kerre, Ghent University, Belgium
Kuan Yew Wong, Universiti Teknologi Malaysia (UTM), Malaysia
Yao Yiping, National University of Defence Technology - Changsha, Hunan, P. R. China

SIMUL Industry/Research Advisory Committee

Tsan-sheng Hsu, Institute of Information Science | Academia Sinica, Taiwan
Letizia Nicoletti, Cal-tek srl, Italy

SIMUL 2018 Technical Program Committee

Kareem Abdelgawad, Audi AG - Ingolstadt, Germany
El-Houssaine Aghezzaf, Ghent University, Belgium
Mikulas Alexik, University of Zilina, Slovak Republic
Ciro Alberto Amaya, University of Los Andes, Bogotá, Colombia
Frédéric Amblard, IRIT | Université Toulouse 1 Capitole, France
Boris Andrievsky, Russian Academy of Sciences, Russia
Chrissanthi Angeli, Piraeus University of Applied Sciences, Greece
Amr Arisha, Dublin Institute of Technology (DIT), Ireland
Alfonso Ariza Quintana, University of Malaga, Spain
Marek Bauer, Politechnika Krakowska, Poland
Ateet Bhalla, Independent Consultant, India
Paul-Antoine Bisgambiglia, University of Corsica Pasquale Paoli, France
Paolo Bocciarelli, University of Rome Tor Vergata, Italy
Christos Bouras, University of Patras | Computer Technology Institute & Press «Diophantus», Greece
Benjamin Camus, Inria | IRISA, Rennes, France
Paula M. Castro, University of A Coruña, Spain
Eugene Ch'ng, University of Nottingham Ningbo, China
Federico Ciccozzi, Mälardalen University, Sweden
Franco Cicirelli, ICAR-CNR, Italy
Duilio Curcio, University of Calabria (CS), Italy
Andrea D'Ambrogio, University of Roma "Tor Vergata", Italy
Gabriele D'Angelo, University of Bologna, Italy
Maryam Davoudpour, *Ryerson* University, Canada
Luis Antonio De Santa-Eulalia, Université de Sherbrooke, Canada
Jorge de Jesus Lozoya Santos, Universidad de Monterrey, Mexico

Tuğçe Demirdelen, Adana Science and Technology University, Turkey
Pierangelo Di Sanzo, DIAG - Sapienza University of Rome, Italy
Alexander Ditter, Friedrich-Alexander University Erlangen-Nürnberg (FAU), Germany
Anatoli Djanatliev, University of Erlangen-Nuremberg, Germany
Atalan Dogan, Anadolu University, Turkey
Julie Dugdale, University Grenoble Alps, France
Vinod Dumblekar, MANTIS, India
Rémy Dupas, University of Bordeaux, France
Amr Eltawil, School of Innovative Design Engineering | Egypt Japan University of Science and Technology, Egypt
Sabeur Elkosantini, University of Monastir, Tunisia
Diego Encinas, Informatics Research Institute LIDI – National University of La Plata (UNLP), Argentina
Fouad Erchiqui, Université du Québec en Abitibi-Témiscamingue, Canada
Zuhal Erden, ATILIM University, Ankara, Turkey
Sigrid Ewert, University of the Witwatersrand, Johannesburg, South Africa
Bernhard Fechner, FernUniversität in Hagen, Germany
Ian Flood, University of Florida, USA
Adrian Florea, 'Lucian Blaga' University of Sibiu, Romania
Romain Franceschini, University of Corsica, France
Sibylle Fröschle, OFFIS e.V. - Institut für Informatik, Germany
José Manuel Galán, Universidad de Burgos, Spain
Héctor Miguel Gastélum González, Tecnológico Nacional de México - Instituto Tecnológico de Tlajomulco, Mexico
Simon Genser, VIRTUAL VEHICLE Research Center, Austria
Charlotte Gerritsen, Vrije Universiteit Amsterdam, Netherlands
Katja Gilly, Universidad Miguel Hernández, Spain
Luis Gomes, Universidade Nova de Lisboa, Portugal
Antoni Grau, Technical University of Catalonia - UPC, Barcelona, Spain
Petr Hanacek, Brno University, Czech Republic
Magdalena Hańderek, Cracow University of Technology, Poland
Thomas Hanne, University of Applied Sciences and Arts Northwestern Switzerland / Institute for Information Systems, Switzerland
Houcine Hassan, Universitat Politecnica de Valencia, Spain
Frank Herrmann, OTH Regensburg, Germany
Celso Hirata, Instituto Tecnologico de Aeronautica, Brazil
Tsan-sheng Hsu, Institute of Information Science | Academia Sinica, Taiwan
Xiaolin Hu, Georgia State University, USA
Marc-Philippe Huget, Polytech Annecy-Chambery-LISTIC | University of Savoie, France
Mauro Iacono, Università degli Studi della Campania "Luigi Vanvitelli", Italy
Joshua Ignatius, University of Warwick, Coventry, UK
Emilio Insfran, Universitat Politecnica de Valencia, Spain
Emilio Jiménez Macías, University of La Rioja, Spain
Maria João Viamonte, Institute of Engineering (ISEP) - Polytechnic Institute of Porto (IPP), Portugal
Zsolt Csaba Johanyák, Pallasz Athéné University, Hungary
Eugene B. John, The University of Texas at San Antonio, USA
Imed Kacem, LCOMS - Université de Lorraine, France
Waldemar Karwowski, University of Central Florida, USA
Hamdi Kavak, Old Dominion University, USA

Peter Kemper, College of William and Mary, USA
Etienne Kerre, Ghent University, Belgium
Daria Kolmakova, Samara National Research University, Russia
Petia Koprinkova-Hristova, Institute of Information and Communication Technologies | Bulgarian Academy of Sciences, Bulgaria
Dmitry G. Korzun, Petrozavodsk State University | Institute of Mathematics and Information Technology, Russia
Harald Köstler, Friedrich-Alexander University Erlangen-Nürnberg, Germany
Claudia Krull, Institut für Simulation und Graphik | Otto-von-Guericke-Universität Magdeburg, Germany
Anatoly Kurkovsky, Georgia Gwinnett College - Greater Atlanta University System of Georgia, USA
Massimo La Scala, Politecnico di Bari, Italy
Fedor Lehocki, Slovak University of Technology in Bratislava, Slovak Republic
Iris Lorscheid, Institute of Management Accounting and Simulation (MACCS) | Hamburg University of Technology, Germany
Edwin Lughofer, Johannes Kepler University Linz, Austria
Emilio Luque, University Autonoma of Barcelona (UAB), Spain
Johannes Lüthi, Fachhochschule Kufstein Tirol University of Applied Sciences, Austria
Jose Machado, Universidade do Minho, Portugal
Leandros Maglaras, De Montfort University, UK
Eda Marchetti, CNR-ISTI, Pisa, Italy
Martin Margala, University of Massachusetts Lowell, USA
Goreti Marreiros, ISEP/IPP - Engineering Institute – Polytechnic of Porto, Portugal
Nuno Melão, Polytechnic Institute of Viseu, Portugal
Hugo Meyer, University of Amsterdam, Netherlands
Adel Mhamdi, RWTH Aachen University, Germany
Bożena Mielczarek, Wroclaw University of Science and Technology, Poland
Francisco José Monaco, University of São Paulo, Brazil
Sébastien Monnet, University Savoie Mont Blanc, France
Roberto Montemanni, Dalle Molle Institute for Artificial Intelligence (IDSIA) | University of Applied Sciences of Southern Switzerland (SUPSI), Switzerland
Paulo Moura Oliveira, UTAD University / INESC-TEC, Portugal
Ivan Mura, Universidad de los Andes, Colombia
Aziz Naamana, LSIS - Marseille, France
Nazmun Nahar, University of Jyvaskyla, Finland
Viorel Nicolau, "Dunarea de Jos" University of Galati, Romania
Letizia Nicoletti, Cal-tek srl, Italy
Libero Nigro, Universitá della Calabria, Italy
Halit Oguztuzun, Middle East Technical University, Turkey
Aida Omerovic, SINTEF, Norway
Tuncer Ören, University of Ottawa, Canada
Nunzia Palmieri, University of Calabria, Italy
Vitalii Pazdrii, Company of Intellectual Technology / Kyiv National Economic University, Ukraine
Witold Pedrycz, University of Alberta, Canada
Laurent Pérochon, VetAgro Sup | Université Clermont Auvergne, France
François Pinet, Irstea, France
Katalin Popovici, The MathWorks Inc., USA
Antoni Portero, IT4Innovations national supercomputing center VŠB – Technical University of Ostrava, Czech Republic

Tomas Potuzak, NTIS – European Center of Excellence / University of West Bohemia Plzen, Czech Republic
Francesco Quaglia, Università di Roma "Tor Vergata", Italy
Mustafa Rafique, IBM Research, Ireland
Arash Ramezani, University of the Federal Armed Forces in Hamburg, Germany
Barbara Re, University of Camerino, Italy
Sven Reissmann, Fulda University of Applied Sciences - University Datacenter, Germany
Roberto Revetria, University of Genoa, Italy / Bauman State University, Moscow, Russian Federation / MEVB Consulting GmbH, Olten, Switzerland
José L. Risco Martín, Complutense University of Madrid, Spain
Paola Rizzi, University of L'Aquila, Italy
Rosaldo J. F. Rossetti, Universidade do Porto, Portugal
Hendrik Rothe, Helmut-Schmidt-Universität/ Universität der Bundeswehr Hamburg, Germany
Julio Sahuquillo Borrás, Universitat Politècnica de València, Spain
Victorino Sanz Prat, ETSI Informática - UNED Madrid, Spain
Mahdiyar Sarayloo, Università Politecnica delle Marche, Italy
Michael Schluse, RWTH Aachen University, Germany
Gerald Schweiger, TU Graz | Institute for software technology, Austria
Paulo Jorge Sequeira Gonçalves, Instituto Politécnico de Castelo Branco, Portugal
Frank Shi, University of California, Irvine, USA
Alireza Shojaei, University of Florida, USA
Yuri N. Skiba, Universidad Nacional Autónoma de México, Mexico
Azeddien Sllame, University of Tripoli, Libya
Giandomenico Spezzano, University of Calabria, Italy
Renata Spolon Lobato, UNESP - São Paulo State University, Brazil
Roberta Spolon, Universidade Estadual Paulista (UNESP), Brazil
Vlado Stankovski, University of Ljubljana, Slovenia
Mu-Chun Su, National Central University, Taiwan
Halina Tarasiuk, Institute of Telecommunications - Warsaw University of Technology, Poland
Pietro Terna, University of Torino, Italy
Flávio Torres Filho, Federal Institute of Paraíba (IFPB), Brazil
Klaus G. Troitzsch, Universität Koblenz-Landau, Germany
Kay Tucci, SUMA-CESIMO | Universidad de Los Andes, Mérida, Venezuela
Andrea Tundis, Technische Universität Darmstadt (TUDA), Germany
Antonio Virdis, University of Pisa, Italy - Dipartimento di Ingegneria dell'Informazione
Alfonso Urquía, UNED, Spain
Durk-Jouke van der Zee, University of Groningen, Netherlands
Svetlana Vasileva-Boyadzhieva, Varna University of Management, Bulgaria
Manuel Villen-Altamirano, Universidad de Málaga, Spain
Vasiliki Vita, ASPETE - School of Pedagogical and Technological Education, Athens, Greece
Jingjing Wang, Binghamton University, USA
Shengyong Wang, University of Akron, USA
Frank Werner, Otto-von-Guericke University Magdeburg, Germany
Edward Williams, University of Michigan – Dearborn, USA
Kuan Yew Wong, Universiti Teknologi Malaysia (UTM), Malaysia
Ramin Yahyapour, Gesellschaft für wissenschaftliche Datenverarbeitung mbH Göttingen (GWDG), Germany
Zhen Yan, Guangxi Normal University, China

Yao Yiping, National University of Defence Technology - Changsha, Hunan, P. R. China
Levent Yilmaz, Auburn University, USA
Behrouz Zarei, University of Tehran, Iran
František Zbořil, Brno University of Technology, Czech Republic
Soraya Zertal, Université de Versailles, France

Copyright Information

For your reference, this is the text governing the copyright release for material published by IARIA.

The copyright release is a transfer of publication rights, which allows IARIA and its partners to drive the dissemination of the published material. This allows IARIA to give articles increased visibility via distribution, inclusion in libraries, and arrangements for submission to indexes.

I, the undersigned, declare that the article is original, and that I represent the authors of this article in the copyright release matters. If this work has been done as work-for-hire, I have obtained all necessary clearances to execute a copyright release. I hereby irrevocably transfer exclusive copyright for this material to IARIA. I give IARIA permission or reproduce the work in any media format such as, but not limited to, print, digital, or electronic. I give IARIA permission to distribute the materials without restriction to any institutions or individuals. I give IARIA permission to submit the work for inclusion in article repositories as IARIA sees fit.

I, the undersigned, declare that to the best of my knowledge, the article is does not contain libelous or otherwise unlawful contents or invading the right of privacy or infringing on a proprietary right.

Following the copyright release, any circulated version of the article must bear the copyright notice and any header and footer information that IARIA applies to the published article.

IARIA grants royalty-free permission to the authors to disseminate the work, under the above provisions, for any academic, commercial, or industrial use. IARIA grants royalty-free permission to any individuals or institutions to make the article available electronically, online, or in print.

IARIA acknowledges that rights to any algorithm, process, procedure, apparatus, or articles of manufacture remain with the authors and their employers.

I, the undersigned, understand that IARIA will not be liable, in contract, tort (including, without limitation, negligence), pre-contract or other representations (other than fraudulent misrepresentations) or otherwise in connection with the publication of my work.

Exception to the above is made for work-for-hire performed while employed by the government. In that case, copyright to the material remains with the said government. The rightful owners (authors and government entity) grant unlimited and unrestricted permission to IARIA, IARIA's contractors, and IARIA's partners to further distribute the work.

Application of Complex Systems Architecting Approach to Develop a Digital Twin

Application: Phosphate mining site of Benguerir

Makouar Kaltoum, Deshayes Laurent
ILO
UM6P
Benguérir, Morocco
Email : Kaltoum.makouar@um6p.ma
Email : Deshayes.laurent@um6p.ma

Mouchtachi Ahmed, Aitelmahjoub Abdelhafid
L.I.S.S.I.E.E
ENSAM
Casablanca, Morocco
Email: ahmedmouchtachi@yahoo.fr
Email: aitelmajoub@gmail.com

Abstract— **The aim of this paper is to present the application of complex systems architecting approach in the development of the digital twin through a use case of an industrial process: phosphate mining site of Benguérir. We introduce the digital twin concept and its influence on the development of manufacturing processes. Further, we present the complex systems engineering approach and its added value to the design and the manipulation of systems with a higher level of complexity, and how this approach allows designing a digital twin model of the mining site. Previous work undertook the digital twin concept and its benefits on industry without mentioning an efficient method to develop it. To realize our vision to design the digital twin of the mining site of Benguérir, we used SysML diagrams to model the solution based on the three visions of the complex systems engineering: the operational vision, the functional vision and the constructional vision.**

Keywords- Industry 4.0; digital twin; simulators; complex systems engineering; mining site; fixed infrastructures.

I. INTRODUCTION

The fixed infrastructures of the mining site are a main process in its value chain, whose function is the physical treatment of the extracted product. It consists in separating rocks from valuable product and the transfer of this product to the other sites (chemical treatments); this process is composed of three units:

- Stone removal unit: The trucks bring the product (the phosphate) from the field, and put it into two hoppers, then it is screened, the rocks are crushed and sent to a waste rock storage and the product is sent to the next unit via conveyors.
- Screening unit: A second screen is necessary; the unit contains five screens and five hoppers; the product is now sent via conveyors to the loading unit.
- Loading unit: The product is stored and then loaded in specific wagons depending on the quality, the type and the quantity demanded from the customers.

The industrial manufacturing and, of course, the mining sites are getting into a deep transformation, which considers digital technologies getting into industrial equipment. This is the fourth industrial revolution, called Industry4.0. It is characterized by the fusion of virtual world of internet and the real industrial facilities.

There are three big challenges to face, in order to be able to pursue this transformation:

- Training: Industry 4.0's transformation requires not only to change equipment but also to change minds, operators should be aware of the new technologies and their use.
- Test and verification: The operator needs to change the configurations, edit the program, upgrade the system or maintain a new equipment, and this without any risk or failure, so, the operator must simulate and test the modification before implementing it in the real process.
- R&D: Engineers and researchers need to develop algorithms and new methods based on the data collected from the field and test the results and algorithms.

To face those challenges, and pursue the change, the Polytechnic University of Mohammed VI and the mining site of the Office Chérifien des Phosphates (OCP) adopted the digital twin concept to deal with the issues discussed before.

The digital twin is the virtual representation of a real process, product or service [1]; it contains of real time simulators and this representation is a complex system since it must be a very close model of the real system. Furthermore, a well-defined design process should be used in order to collect all requirements from all stakeholders. The complex engineering system approach provides a structured and flexible modelling methodology in order to implement and develop a clear functional architecture.

The aim of this paper is to present the impact of complex systems architecting approach in developing the digital twin of the mining site.

After first describing the principles of systems engineering approach and the digital twin concept, this paper then demonstrates how this approach is an effective methodological support and allows an early detection of possible weaknesses during initial design stages.

The paper is structured as follows: In Section 2, a state of art will be presented, then Section 3 is dedicated to the definition of digital twin concept and its advantages. Furthermore, the complex systems architecting method is presented is Section 4, while Section 5 will present the application of the complex systems architecting method in the process of the mining site and results of this work, and we conclude with a conclusion and perspectives of the work.

II. State of Art

Different understandings of the digital twin can be observed in industrial practice. In this regard, it has been argued that Parametric Technology Corporation (PTC) is focusing on establishing a link between the virtual product model and the physical part to increase the manufacturing flexibility and competitiveness, while Dassault Systèmes targets the product design performance. Moreover, the digital twin understanding of General Electric focuses on forecasting the health and performance of their products over lifetime, whereas SIEMENS strives for improved efficiency and quality in manufacturing. TESLA aims at developing a digital twin for every built car, hence enabling synchronous data transmission between the car and the factory, while other companies increasingly use complex product models to boost the immersion in virtual and augmented reality applications [2].

To develop a flexible digital twin framework and satisfy the multiple understandings, a developed architecting method should be adopted, and as the system is complex and provides many parameters, this work proposes the complex systems architecting method to model and implement the digital twin based on simulators.

The design and development of a system indeed requires the contribution of various processes, stakeholders and techniques. Each person often concentrates on a specific aspect of the system without any perspective on the other aspects: designers have an architectural and functional vision of the system, the manufacturing team considers a system as an element to be integrated in the assembly line, the procurement department views it as a list of supplies to be purchased. Complex systems engineering thus enables a global view of the system to guarantee the consistency of specific contributions to the system; it takes into account the whole life cycle of the system including the definition of customer requirements, design, production, and marketing. It defines the most effective methods and means for satisfying the technical and organizational requirements which, in practice, means satisfying cost, time and productivity constraints. The challenge of complex systems engineering is to design and product the best system to meet a customer's requirements with the most efficient control of deadlines and costs. As system complexity continues to increase, systems engineers now use modelling techniques to guarantee that specification and design models are correctly built and can be easily communicated to the development teams [3].

The objective of the work described in this paper is to demonstrate the advantages of using recommended methodology for the development of complex systems.

III. Digital Twin Concept

First, the project of the digital twin (DT) was originated in the Institute of Automation, Measurement and Applied Informatics of the faculty of Mechanical Engineering of the Slovak University of Technology in Bratislava [4]. The DT is one of the main concepts associated with the new industrial revolution, Industry 4.0. Manufacturers are taking a more systems-design approach by implementing rigorous systems-design processes that accommodate the complexities of developing multi-disciplinary systems. Digital twins are at the core of this development process [5].

The digital twin can allow companies to have a complete digital footprint of their products from design and development through the end of the product life cycle. Digital twins are designed to model complicated assets or processes that interact in many ways with their environments for which it is difficult to predict outcomes over an entire product life cycle, and to solve physical issues faster by detecting them sooner, predict outcomes to a much higher degree of accuracy, design and build better products, and, ultimately, better serve their customers [6].

IV. Complex Systems Engineering Approach

Complex systems engineering approach is the whole activity that allows to design an optimal system to meet a need. It is based on system vision that includes multiple parameters, the multidisciplinary aspect, the life cycle and the use cases. It consists of establishing the functional and physical compatibility of a system with the needs and the constraints

Systems engineering approach enables engineering organizations to proceed toward the design of complex systems and its impact across multiple engineering disciplines: mechanical, electrical, and software. With this approach, customer requirements are defined early in the development cycle and are implemented through design and system validation—from concept to operation [7]. This approach is based on three essential visions: Operational vision, functional vision and constructional vision.

- Operational Vision: The operational vision provides "black box" models [8] of a given system where one describes the interactions and the interfaces of a system of interest with its environment. Its core motivation is to understand the "Why" – of the system.
- Functional Vision: The core notion of the functional vision is to understand the "what" of the system, it functions, and the main mission is to understand deeply what does the system without however knowing at this point how it is concretely structured.
- Constructional Vision: The aim is to describe all concrete hardware, software and human-ware components of a system with their interactions; all constructional concepts, such as configuration, constructional scenarios or constructional objects are again uniquely referring to the system of interest without involving any external system [9].

V. Application & Results

In order to implement the complex systems engineering approach, we have employed the SysML modeling language to develop different diagrams for each vision.

The results of applying each vision are the operational, the functional and the constructional diagrams; those diagrams will facilitate to develop the digital twin of the mining site. This method is characterized by high precision, accurate functioning and various configurations.

A. *Operational vision*

The aim of the operational vision is to identify the multiple users of our system and its environment, also to understand the stakeholders and the interactions between them. It facilitates to design our system with high precision because a misunderstanding or an error occurred during the operational architecture process may lead to costly and disastrous consequences on our system under development.

Fig.1 below describes the use cases of our system. The digital twin of the OCP mining site will be used by multiple stakeholders which are: Operators, supervisors, production agents, maintenance agents and office managers. Its use cases are: the test of the configurations, the optimization of process, the simulation of the process, prediction of the system performance, real time monitoring and also for the production management.

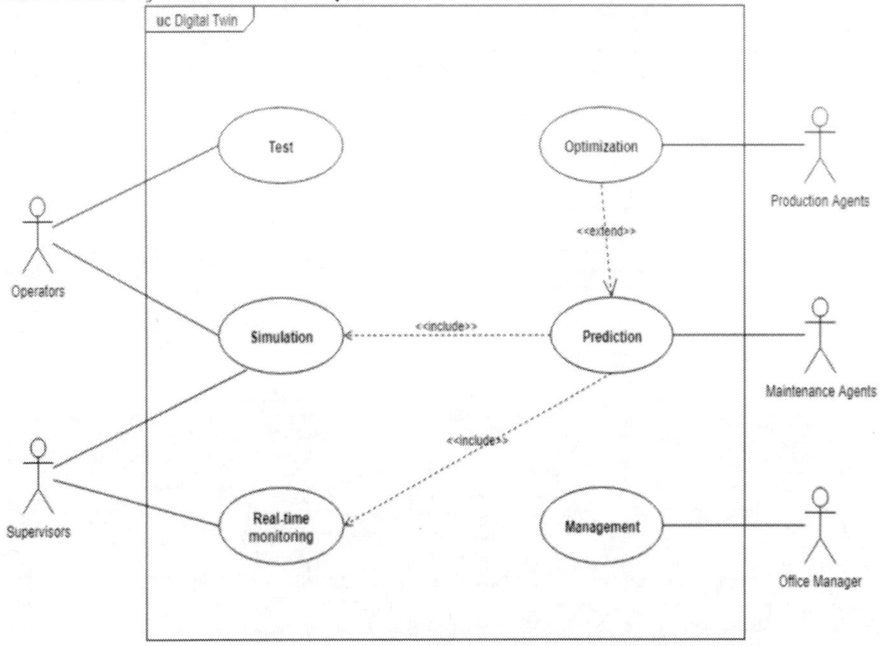

Figure.1: Use cases diagram of the digital twin

B. *Functional vision*

The results of the treatment of this vision are the functional requirements of our system (the digital twin) which are the functional needs of the operators from the field, agents, engineers and office managers. We will present the results of applying the functional vision of complex system engineering to develop the functional diagrams that will serve to develop the digital twin of the mining site.

As mentioned before, requirements engineering is an essential part of systems engineering. Indeed, understanding the need facilitates designing the solution. Every requirement should be S.M.A.R.T: Specific, Measurable, Achievable, Relevant and Traceable [10].

Operators express their needs and the challenges they face by writing texts and classical sentences, e.g., The stacker needs to be automated; the provider of the solution may have different reflections and challenges to design the right and exact solution for the problem. The aim of this work is to identify the real needs of the operators, to model those needs in a flexible way based on a system modeling language and use the requirements model to verify and validate the solution proposed to implement the digital twin.

Fig.2 below describes the functional requirements of our system. Those requirements have been identified from the users of the digital twin. We classified them into four sections: Simulators, Research and development (R&D), Training and test and validation. We have also set the requirements for each section in order to model those requirements in a flexible way.

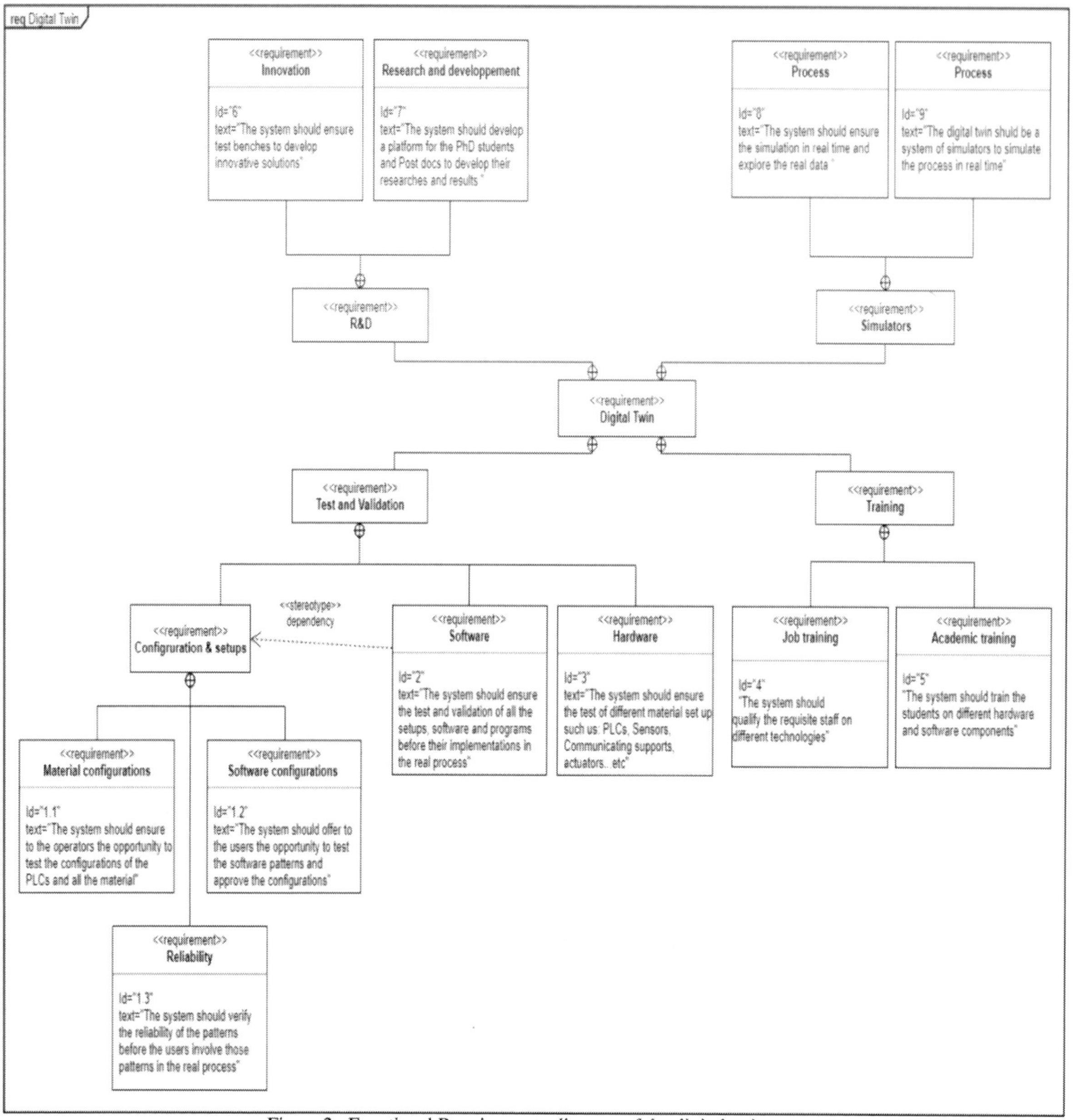

Figure.2: Functional Requirements diagram of the digital twin

C. Constructional vision

Constructional architecture is key since it consolidates all architectural analyses in a concrete vision of the considered system. It makes in particular the synthesis between a top-down design approach, as provided by the systems architecting process, and a bottom-up one, which is typically induced by the constraints due to the existing product architecture or by the new possibilities brought by the advances of technology [11].

Fig.3 shows the definition block diagram of the digital twin. This system is composed of n number of PLCs, motors, actuators, sensors, panels and computers. The definition block diagram shows the components of the digital twin, their parts, their values and the ports of the material and the energy of those components.

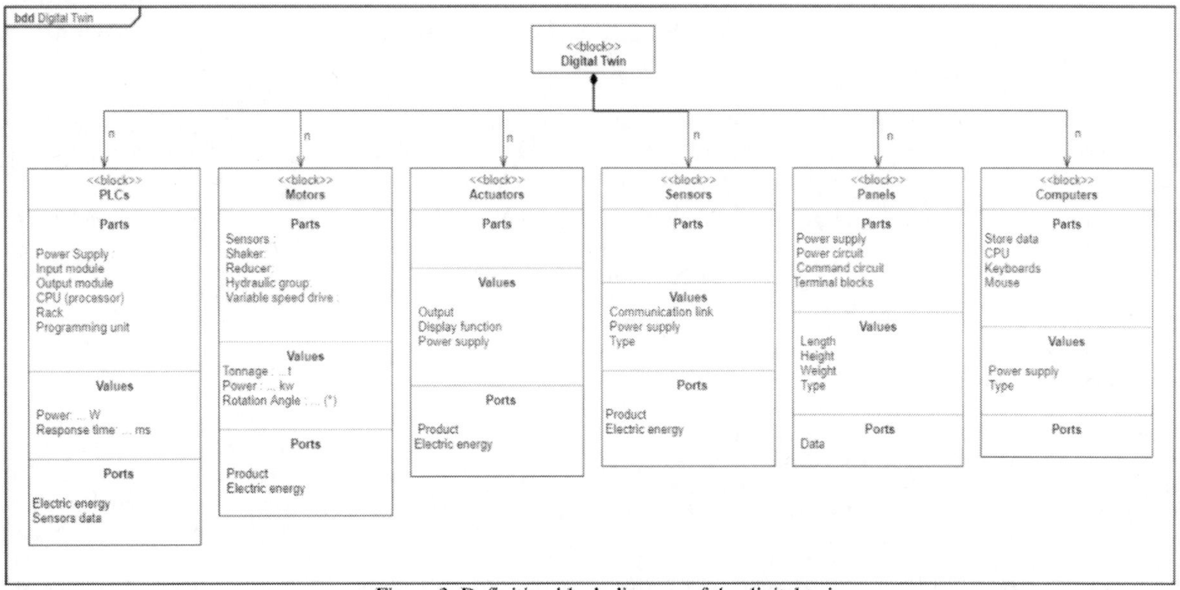

Figure.3. Definition block diagram of the digital twin

Those diagrams will be used to establish the physical architecture of the digital twin of the fixed infrastructures with all the components.

VI. CONCLUSION AND PERSPECTIVES

The mining site of OCP and the Polytechnic University of Mohammed VI are pursuing the digital transformation by developing innovative and advanced solutions for mining and chemical processes. The example of this project is a good demonstration that the complex engineering systems approach is a powerful tool to design future advanced and fully digitalized systems and to optimize existing mining systems. The results obtained in this work, which are the operational, the functional and the constructional diagrams of the digital twin of the mining site will be used to implement our digital twin; they facilitate modeling the global architecture of our system and maintain its flexibility. In addition, it allows to test the automation solutions and advanced technologies implemented in the digital twin and it helps to offer innovative technological solutions in order to implement an advanced model of control and real time monitoring of the mining site.

REFERENCES

[1] E. Negri, L. Fumagalli, and M. Macchi, "A review of the roles of digital twin in CPS-based production systems", Modena, Italy, p. 427, June 2017.

[2] B. Schleich, N. Anwer, L. Mathieu, and S. Wartzack, "Shaping the digital twin for design and production engineering", Germany, p.2, 2017.

[3] G. Auriol, C. Baron, and J. Y. Fourniols, "The advantages of systems engineering standards, a case study of application of the EIA632 standard to design of a small-scale yacht", Toulouse, France, p.2, 2011.

[4] M. Morhàc, M. Moksik, J. Vanchalek, L. Bartalsky, O. Rovny, and D. Sismisova, "The digital twin of an industrial production line within the industry 4.0 concept", Štrbské Pleso, Slovakia, p. 1, June 2017.

[5] P. Goossens, "Industry 4.0 and the Power of the digital twin", Canada, p. 4, September 2017.

[6] A. Parott, L. Warshaw, Deloitte University Press, "Industry 4.0 and the digital twin Manufacturing meets its match",USA, p. 2, May 2017.

[7] EETIndia, "Advantages of systems engineering approach", p. 2, October 2013.

[8] CESAM Community, CESAMES Systems Architecting Method, A Pocket Guide, p. 42, January 2017.

[9] CESAM Community, CESAMES Systems Architecting Method, A Pocket Guide, p. 46, January 2017.

[10] White book, Requirements engineering for an information system, Compliance Consulting, p .11.

[11] CESAM Community, CESAMES Systems Architecting Method, A Pocket Guide, p. 93, January 2017.

Thermal Softening Effects on Simulation Models of Fiber-Reinforced Plastics Under High-Velocity Impact

Arash Ramezani and Hendrik Rothe
Chair of Measurement and Information Technology
University of the Federal Armed Forces
Hamburg, Germany
Email: ramezani@hsu-hh.de, rothe@hsu-hh.de

Abstract*—In the security sector, the partly insufficient safety of people and equipment due to failure of industrial components is an ongoing problem that causes great concern. Since computers and software have spread into all fields of industry, extensive efforts are currently made to improve the safety by applying certain numerical solutions. A fibre-reinforced composite is a promising material for ballistic protection due to its high strength, stiffness and low density. Para-aramid fibre was introduced into the market in the 1970s. These fibres are five times stronger than steel. In more recent years, Ultra-High Molecular Weight Polyethylene (UHMW-PE) fibre has been used in ballistic application owing to certain property advantages. UHMW-PE composites as part of the personal armour system have the potential to provide significant weight savings or improved protection levels over traditional metallic materials. Although already used in different applications, both as spall liners and within complex multi-element/multi-material packages, there is a limited understanding of the mechanisms driving ballistic performance. Existing analysis tools do not allow a good approximation of performance, while existing numerical models are either incapable of accurately capturing the response of thick UHMW-PE composite to ballistic impact or are unsuited to model thick targets. In response, this paper aims to identify the key penetration and failure mechanisms of thick UHMW-PE composites under ballistic impact and develop numerical models that capture these mechanisms and allow accurate prediction of ballistic performance to optimize modern armour systems. An important aspect of impact loading of polyethylene-based composites is their propensity to thermally soften or even melt during a collision due to shock heating. Consequently, this needs to be taken into account in both analytical and computational models. The motivation of this work was to develop a thermal softening model and investigate the effects on existing simulation models.

Keywords-hydrocode analysis; thermal softening; fiber-reinforced plastics; optimization; armor systems; ballistic trials.

I. INTRODUCTION

The object behind combining different materials to form a composite with enhanced properties and synergetic effects is par for the course in nature. A section through a paracortical cell in merino wool or through a bamboo stems exhibits structures similar to the micrograph of a unidirectional Carbon-Fibre-Reinforced Epoxy Resin (CF-EP). Not only in the microstructure can nature be seen as the progenitor of fibre-reinforced plastics, but also in the application of lightweight design principles.

Why material scientists integrate fibers in materials to such advantage can be answered by the following four paradoxes of engineering materials:

- The paradox of the solid material: The actual strength of a solid material is very much lower than the calculated theoretical value.
- The paradox of the fiber form: The strength of a material in fiber form is many times higher than that of the same material in another form, and the thinner the fiber, the greater the strength.
- The paradox of the free clamped length: The shorter the length between the clamps, the greater the strength measured on the test piece.
- The paradox of composites: When taken as a whole, a composite can withstand stresses that would fracture the weaker component, whereas the composite's stronger component can exhibit a greater percentage of its theoretical strength than when loaded singly.

So, the principle of combining different materials to form a composite with enhanced properties is just as common in nature as it is in lightweight engineering. This design method based on nature's example has virtually revolutionized many fields of technology, with the result that they can now utilize the superior properties of high-tensile, lightweight materials for the first time.

This work will focus on fiber-reinforced plastics, more precisely composite armor structures consisting of several layers of UHMW-PE, a promising ballistic armor material due to its high specific strength and stiffness. First numerical approaches are discussed in [1].

UHMW-PE is a thermoplastic polymer made from very long molecular chains of polyethylene. Thermoplastics soften when subjected to heat and so can be repeatedly remoulded. Cut-offs can be remelted and introduced back into the production process. Many thermoplastics are soluble in organic solvents. Thermoplastics can be joined by welding under the application of heat or by the action of solvents [2].

Figure 1 shows the chemical structure of polyethylene, where in UHMW-PE the number of repeated chains (n) is in the order of 10^5, giving rise to molecular weights in the order of 10^6 [3]. As a non-polar molecule, interaction between polyethylene molecules is given by very weak Van der Waals forces.

However, due to the ultra-long polymer chain, significant strength can be derived through a gel spinning process that produces highly oriented and crystalline molecular structures aligned in the spinning direction. The gel spinning process firstly involves dissolving UHMW-PE in a solvent at high temperature. The solution is then pushed through a spinneret to form liquid filament that is then quenched in water to form gel-fibers. These fibers are then drawn in hot air at high strain rates of the order of 1 s^{-1} forming fibers with smooth circular cross-sections approximately 17 μm in diameter [4] with a molecular orientation greater than 95% and a crystallinity of up to 85% [3], see Figure 2.

These fibers are composed of smaller macro-fibrils approximately 0.5 mm to 2 mm in diameter, which in turn are made of micro-fibrils, 20 nm in diameter. Commercial UHMW-PE fiber is manufactured by, amongst others, Dutch State Mines (DSM) and Honeywell under the trade names Dyneema® and Spectra®, respectively. The fibers are used in a variety of applications requiring high specific strength and low weight. This includes high strength ropes and nets, cut-resistant gloves, as well as blast and ballistic protection.

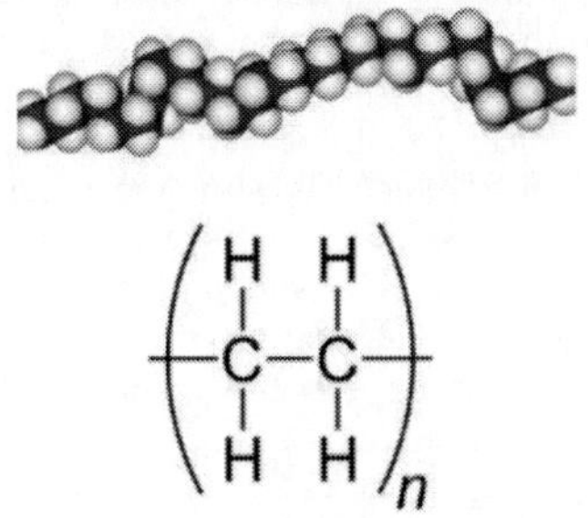

Figure 1. Skeletal formula and spacefill model of a polyethylene.

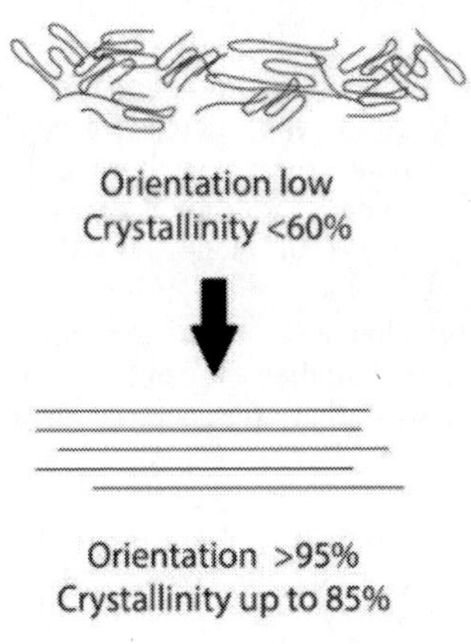

Figure 2. Increase in molecular orientation and crystallinity through gel spinning of UHMW-PE [5].

For ballistic protection applications, the fibers can be woven into fabrics to provide a soft and flexible material or coated in a matrix and aligned to form uni-directional plies, which are then stacked and pressed under temperature and pressure to form rigid laminates.

UHMW-PE composites and fabrics have been shown to be extremely effective against ballistic threats, particularly in weight-critical applications, e.g., personal protection vests and helmets for protection against small calibre threats [6]. The goal is to evaluate the ballistic efficiency of UHMW-PE composite with numerical simulations, promoting an effective development process. Additionally, a thermal softening model is implemented and analyzed.

After a brief introduction and an overview of all state-of-the-art models of fiber-reinforced plastics, the principles of simulation are discussed in Section III, followed by the penetration and perforation principles of composites in Section IV. There is a short section on ballistic trials where the experimental set-up is depicted, followed by Section VI describing the model validation. Section VII presents the analysis with numerical simulations and the results of this work. The paper ends with a concluding paragraph in Section VIII.

II. STATE-OF-THE-ART

The numerical modelling of composite materials under impact can be performed at a constituent level (i.e., explicit modelling of fiber and matrix elements, e.g., [7]), a meso-mechanical level (i.e., consolidated plies or fiber bundles, e.g., [8]), or macromechanically in which the composite laminate is represented as a continuum.

In [9–12], a non-linear orthotropic continuum material model was developed and implemented in a commercial hydrocode (i.e., ANSYS® AUTODYN®) for application with aramid and carbon fiber composites under hypervelocity impact. The non-linear orthotropic material model includes orthotropic coupling of the material volumetric and deviatoric responses, a non-linear Equation of State (EoS), orthotropic hardening, combined stress failure criteria and orthotropic energy-based softening. For more detail refer to [13].

Lässig et al. [14] conducted extensive experimental characterization of Dyneema® HB26 UHMW-PE composite for application in the continuum non-linear orthotropic material model, and validated the derived material parameters through simulation of spherical projectile impacts at hypervelocity.

A number of researchers have applied the non-linear orthotropic model for UHMW-PE composites with varying levels of success (Hayhurst et al. [15], Herlaar et al. [16], Ong et al. [17], Heisserer and Van der Werff [18] and Lässig et al. [14]). Ong et al. [17] assumed material properties of UHMW-PE composite based on those of Kevlar® with some data from literature, which resulted in poor predictions of the penetration behaviour. Hayhurst et al. [15], Herlaar et al. [16], Heisserer and Van der Werff

[18] used material input parameters derived from a range of experiments, and reported better prediction, although the results cannot be independently verified because the material parameters are not provided. Nguyen et al. [19] evaluated and refined the modelling approach and material model parameter set developed in [14] for the simulation of impact events from 400 m/s to 6600 m/s. Across this velocity range, the sensitivity of the numerical output is driven by different aspects of the material model, e.g., the strength model in the ballistic regime and the EoS in the hypervelocity regime.

This paper will present an optimized solution of this problem with an enhanced model for ultra-high molecular weight polyethylene under impact loading. The composite armor structures consisting of several layers of fiber-reinforced plastics are simulated for all current military threats. Following this, a user-defined subroutine was written to incorporate the effects of thermal heating into the material data. This subroutine was then tested iteratively until an appropriate level of thermal softening was accounted for to accurately predict the deformation, damage and residual velocity of a range of target thicknesses and impact velocities.

III. Principles of Simulation

To deal with problems involving the release of a large amount of energy over a very short period of time, e.g., explosions and impacts, there are three approaches: as the problems are highly non-linear and require information regarding material behavior at ultra-high loading rates which is generally not available, most of the work is *experimental* and thus may cause tremendous expenses. *Analytical* approaches are possible if the geometries involved are relatively simple and if the loading can be described through boundary conditions, initial conditions or a combination of the two. *Numerical* solutions are far more general in scope and remove any difficulties associated with geometry [20]. They apply an explicit method and use very small time steps for stable results.

For problems of dynamic fluid-structure interaction and impact, there typically is no single best numerical method which is applicable to all parts of a problem. Techniques to couple types of numerical solvers in a single simulation can allow the use of the most appropriate solver for each domain of the problem.

The goal of this paper is to evaluate a hydrocode, a computational tool for modelling the behavior of continuous media. In its purest sense, a hydrocode is a computer code for modelling fluid flow at all speeds. In essence, the code considers the effect of external and internal forces on a predefined "mesh" of cells [21]. For that reason, a structure will be split into a number of small elements. The elements are connected through their nodes (see Figure 3). The behavior (deflection) of the simple elements is well-known and may be calculated and analyzed using simple equations called shape functions [22].

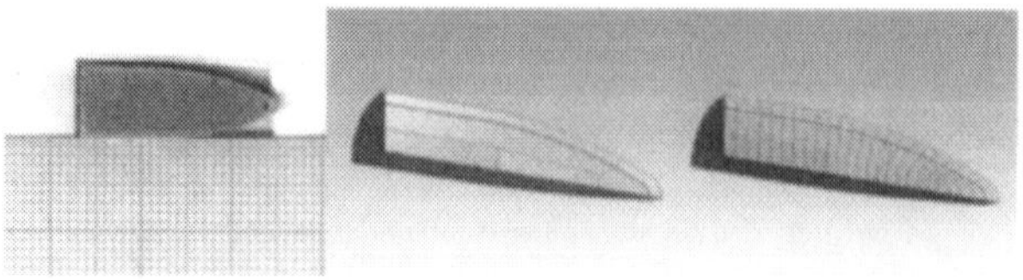

Figure 3. Example grid.

By applying coupling conditions between the elements at their nodes, the overall stiffness of the structure may be built up and the deflection/distortion of any node – and subsequently of the whole structure – can be calculated approximately [23].

A repeatedly used term in this context will be discretization. Its meaning is that equations, formulated to continuously describe a function or functional in space and time, is solved only at certain discrete locations and instants of time [24]. The most commonly used spatial discretization methods are Lagrange, Euler, ALE (a mixture of Lagrange and Euler), and mesh-free methods, such as Smooth Particles Hydrodynamics (SPH) [25].

A. Lagrange

The Lagrange method of space discretization uses a mesh that moves and distorts with the material it models as a result of forces from neighboring elements (meshes are imbedded in material). There is no grid required for the external space, as the conservation of mass is automatically satisfied and material boundaries are clearly defined. This is the most efficient solution methodology with an accurate pressure history definition.

The Lagrange method is most appropriate for representing solids, such as structures and projectiles. If however, there is too much deformation of any element, it results in a very slowly advancing solution and is usually terminated because the smallest dimension of an element results in a time step that is below the threshold level.

B. Euler

The Euler (multi-material) solver utilizes a fixed mesh, allowing materials to flow (advect) from one element to the next (meshes are fixed in space). Therefore, an external space needs to be modeled. Due to the fixed grid, the Euler method avoids problems of mesh distortion and tangling that are prevalent in Lagrange simulations with large flows. The Euler solver is very well-suited for problems involving extreme material movement, such as fluids and gases. To describe solid behavior, additional calculations are required to transport the solid stress tensor and the history of the material through the grid. Euler is generally more computationally intensive than Lagrange and requires a higher resolution (smaller elements) to accurately capture sharp pressure peaks that often occur with shock waves.

C. ALE

The ALE method of space discretization is a hybrid of the Lagrange and Euler methods. It allows redefining the grid continuously in arbitrary and predefined ways as the calculation proceeds, which effectively provides a continuous rezoning facility. Various predefined grid motions can be specified, such as free (Lagrange), fixed (Euler), equipotential, equal spacing, and others. The ALE method can model solids as well as liquids. The advantage of ALE is the ability to reduce and sometimes eliminate difficulties caused by severe mesh distortions encountered by the Lagrange method, thus allowing a calculation to continue efficiently. However, compared to Lagrange, an additional computational step of rezoning is employed to move the grid and remap the solution onto a new grid [26].

D. SPH

The mesh-free Lagrangian method of space discretization (or SPH method) is a particle-based solver and was initially used in astrophysics. The particles are imbedded in material and they are not only interacting mass points but also interpolation points used to calculate the value of physical variables based on the data from neighboring SPH particles, scaled by a weighting function. Because there is no grid defined, distortion and tangling problems are avoided as well. Compared to the Euler method, material boundaries and interfaces in the SPH are rather well defined and material separation is naturally handled. Therefore, the SPH solver is ideally suited for certain types of problems with extensive material damage and separation, such as cracking. This type of response often occurs with brittle materials and hypervelocity impacts. However, mesh-free methods, such as Smooth Particles Hydrodynamics, can be less efficient than mesh-based Lagrangian methods with comparable resolution.

ANSYS Autodyn lets you select from these different solver technologies so he most effective solver can be used for a given part of the model. Figure 4 gives a short overview of the solver technologies mentioned above. The crucial factor is the grid that causes different outcomes.

Using a CAD-neutral environment that supports bidirectional, direct, and associative interfaces with CAD systems, the geometry can be optimized successively [28]. Therefore, several runs are necessary: from modelling to calculation to the evaluation and subsequent improvement of the model.

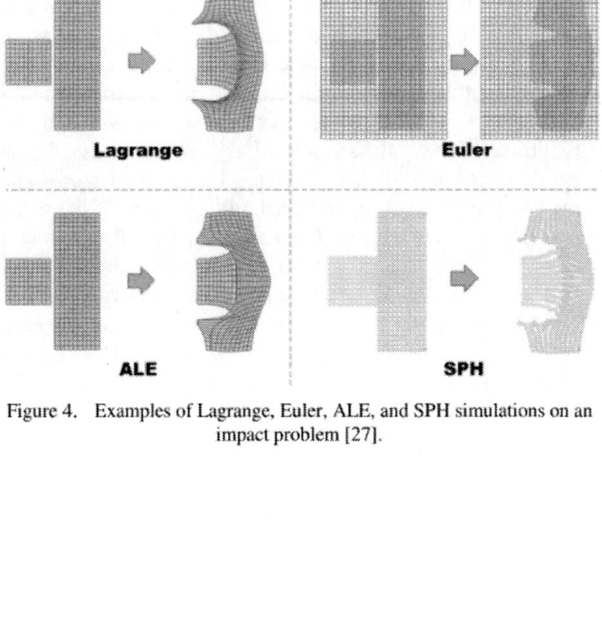

Figure 4. Examples of Lagrange, Euler, ALE, and SPH simulations on an impact problem [27].

AUTODYN's interaction logic enables automatic communication between the various solvers coexisting within the same model. Lagrange-Lagrange, SPH-Lagrange and Euler-Lagrange interactions can all be created within the model in a simple and intuitive manner. This allows fluid structure interactions to be simulated. Furthermore, it can be combined with AUTODYN's extensive remapping and dezoning capabilities between the different solvers and a wide range of erosion settings. It is also possible to retain inertia of eroded material. In this case, the mass and momentum of the free node is retained and can be involved in subsequent impact events to transfer momentum in the system.

IV. Penetration and Perforation of Composites

Composites have arguably been used as armor materials since the middle ages. Advantages of using composite materials are their relatively low density, their tailorable properties, and fair to high strength. The disadvantages of composites are the inconsistency of hand lay-up, the dependency of strength on manufacturing process, and the somewhat expensive nature of their manufacture. Additionally, composites pose a problem to the designers because they are difficult to model.

Composites resist penetration primarily by dissipating energy. Because of the complex structure of the material, this energy dissipation manifests itself in the failure of portions of the laminate, fiber breakage, matrix cracking, and delamination. Since composite properties can vary from isotropic to a complicated anisotropic, the behavior will depend upon the configuration.

In chopped fiber composites, the material properties are usually isotropic. A notable exception to this is in injection moldings where the fibers tend to align with the flow directions near mold gate areas or areas of higher velocity flow. An isotropic composite is usually treated as we do a metal and those formulas should work well.

Continuous fiber composites behave differently from metallic plates. A typical load-displacement curve is shown in Figure 5. In this figure, after an initial delamination point, where the load carrying capability is degraded, we see increases and decreases in load carrying ability based on successive delaminations of material followed by a final plug shear out. This delamination actually promotes energy dissipation by forcing the fibers to elongate. In many composites, shear failure of the fibers, as well as tensile failures dominate during an impact [29].

It is extremely difficult to obtain an analytical model for the penetration of continuous fiber composites. This is due to the change of energy dissipation as the composite is damaged. Finite element methods have been utilized to determine limit velocities, but there are nuances to each analysis that must be explained. Section II presents a general view of all state-of-the-art models of fiber-reinforced plastics.

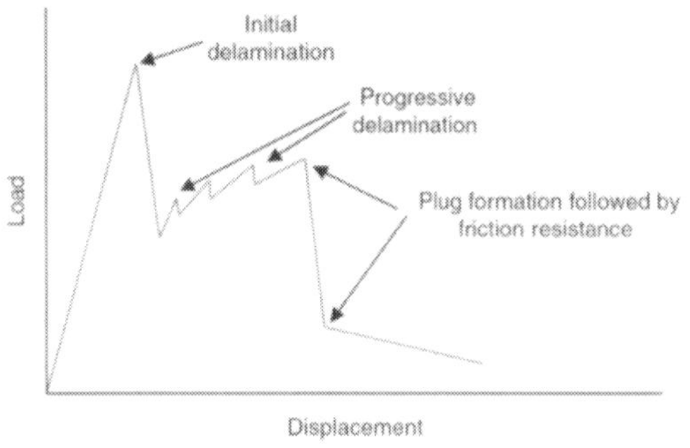

Figure 5. Load–displacement curve for a typical continuous fiber reinforced composite.

The first issue that must be dealt with is how to handle the damage and its effect on the remaining strength of the composite. Some researchers have actually modeled each lamina with its correct directional properties and assumed a failure criterion based on interlaminar shear strength [30]. When the interlaminar shear strength is exceeded, the layer no longer supports shear and the overall bending stiffness is reduced. This can be accounted for explicitly having the model change internal constraints between layers or implicitly by tracking the overall smeared bending stiffness of the composite and reducing it based on the lamina that failed. Another means of handling the behavior of the composite is to average the stiffness change because of the progressive failure of lamina as shown in Figure 6. The issue with this approach is that test data from some sort of penetration event is required.

A second issue with analyzing fiber reinforced composites is the actual failure of the fibers themselves. The fibers can themselves delaminate from the matrix. They can also fail in tension and are usually very sensitive to fracture. These issues of necessity complicate the analysis.

After extensive work in the area of composite materials under impact loads, the following observations regarding their behavior were made: First, delaminations tend to prefer moving along the fiber direction. Additionally, compression of the composite material (e.g., at clamped locations) tends to suppress delamination, as one would expect. The extent of delamination increases linearly as the distal surface is approached if perforation occurs.

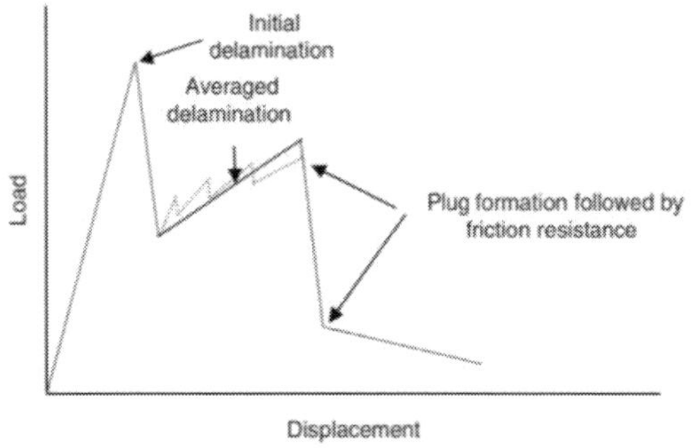

Figure 6. Load–displacement curve for a typical fiber reinforced composite modeled with averaged properties after initial delamination.

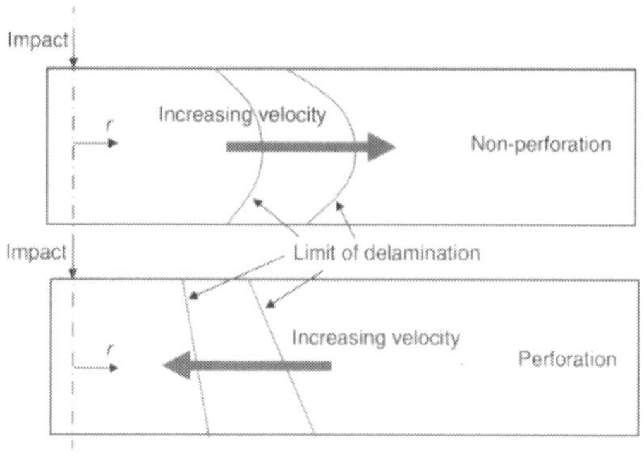

Figure 7. Extent of delamination in a composite with respect to increasing velocity during both perforating and nonperforating impacts.

However, the delamination increases then decreases if no penetration occurred. As the impact velocity increases, the delamination decreases indicating that the bending of the target becomes less significant. This is shown in Figure 7.

V. Ballistic Trials

Ballistics is an essential component for the evaluation of our results. Here, terminal ballistics is the most important sub-field. It describes the interaction of a projectile with its target. Terminal ballistics is relevant for both small and large caliber projectiles. The task is to analyze and evaluate the impact and its various modes of action. This will provide information on the effect of the projectile and the extinction risk.

The science and engineering of impacting bodies have a large range of applications depending on their type and their impact velocities. At very low velocities, these impacts can be limited to the elastic range of response, with practically no damage to the impacted bodies. In contrast, at very high impact velocities these bodies experience gross deformation, local melting, and even total disintegration upon impact. Various scientific and engineering disciplines are devoted to specific areas in this field such as: vehicle impacts, rain erosion, armor and anti-armor design, spacecraft protection against meteorites and the impact of planets by large meteors at extremely high velocities.

Given that a projectile strikes a target, compressive waves propagate into both the projectile and the target. Relief waves propagate inward from the lateral free surfaces of the penetrator, cross at the centerline, and generate a high tensile stress. If the impact was normal, we would have a two-dimensional stress state. If the impact was oblique, bending stresses will be generated in the penetrator. When the compressive wave reached the free surface of the target, it would rebound as a tensile wave. The target may fracture at this point. The projectile may change direction if it perforates (usually towards the normal of the target surface).

Because of the differences in target behavior based on the proximity of the distal surface, we must categorize targets into four broad groups. A semi-infinite target is one where there is no influence of distal boundary on penetration. A thick target is one in which the boundary influences penetration after the projectile is some distance into the target. An intermediate thickness target is a target where the boundaries exert influence throughout the impact. Finally, a thin target is one in which stress or deformation gradients are negligible throughout the thickness.

There are several methods by which a target will fail when subjected to an impact. The major variables are the target and penetrator material properties, the impact velocity, the projectile shape (especially the ogive), the geometry of the target supporting structure, and the dimensions of the projectile and target.

In order to develop a numerical model, a ballistic test program is necessary. The ballistic trials are thoroughly documented and analyzed – even fragments must be collected. They provide information about the used armor and the projectile behavior after fire, which must be consistent with the simulation results (see Figure 8).

Several experiments have to be performed to create a data set for the numerical simulations. Ballistic tests are recorded with high-speed videos and analyzed afterwards. The experimental set-up is shown in Figure 9.

The camera system is a PHANTOM v1611 that enables fast image rates up to 646,000 frames per second (fps) at full resolution of 1280 x 800 pixels. The use of a polarizer and a neutral density filter is advisable, so that waves of some polarizations can be blocked while the light of a specific polarization can be passed.

Several targets of different laminate configurations were tested to assess the ballistic limit (V_{50}). The ballistic limit is considered the velocity required for a particular projectile to reliably (at least 50% of the time) penetrate a particular piece of material [30]. After the impact, the projectile is examined regarding any kind of change it might have undergone.

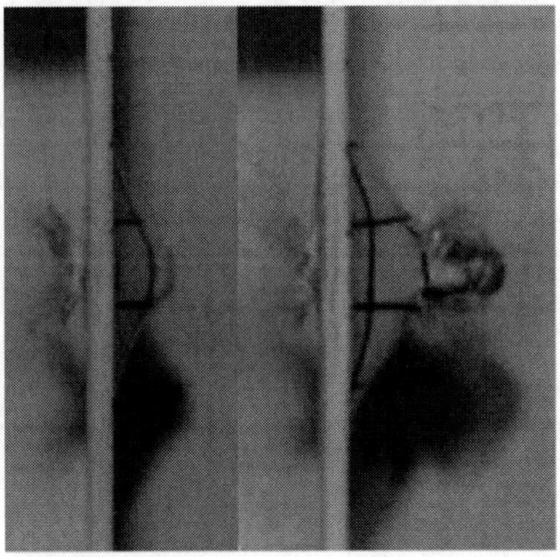

Figure 8. Ballistic tests and the analysis of fragments after 47 μs (left) and 88 μs (right).

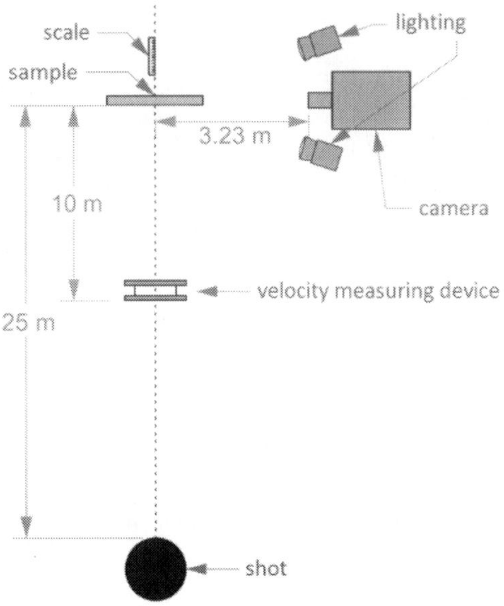

Figure 9. Experimental set-up.

The damage propagation is analyzed using the software called COMEF [31], image processing software for highly accurate measuring functions. The measurement takes place via setting measuring points manually on the monitor. Area measurement is made by the free choice of grey tones (0…255). Optionally the object with the largest surface area can be recognized automatically as object. Smaller particles within the same grey tone range as the sample under test are automatically ignored by this filter.

VI. MODEL VALIDATION

Experimental characterisation of the ballistic performance of UHMW-PE composite can be prohibitively expensive, so it is highly desirable to establish computationally efficient numerical models that accurately predict the ballistic response of the material. First, existing models should be validated.

A. *Resources*

In [19], numerical simulations of 15 kg/m^2 Dyneema® HB26 panels impacted by 6 mm diameter aluminum spheres between 2052 m/s to 6591 m/s were shown to provide very good agreement with experimental measurements of the panel ballistic limit and residual velocities, see Figure 10. The modelling approach and material parameter set from [14] were applied to simulate impact experiments at velocities in the ballistic regime (here considered as < 1000 m/s). Lambert-Jonas parameters (a, p, V_{bl}) are provided in the legend.

In Figure 11, the results of modelling impact of 20 mm fragment simulating projectiles (FSPs) against 10 mm thick Dyneema® HB26 are shown. The model shows a significant under prediction of the ballistic limit, 236 m/s compared to 394 m/s.

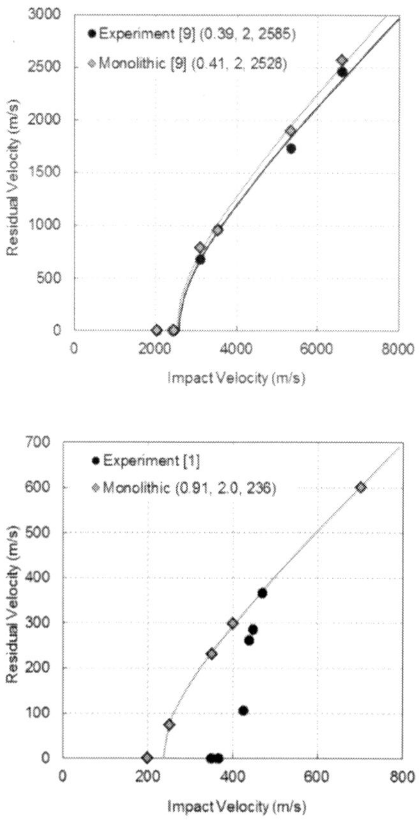

Figure 10. Experimental and numerical impact residual velocity results for impact of 6 mm diameter aluminum spheres (above) and 20 mm FSP (below) against 10 mm thick HB26 at normal incidence.

B. Method

The FSP material was modelled as Steel S-7 from the AUTODYN library using a linear EoS and the Johnson-Cook strength model [32]. The aluminum sphere was modelled using AL1100-O from the AUTODYN library that uses a shock EoS and the Steinburg Guinan strength model [33]. The master-slave contact algorithm was used to detect contact between the target and projectile.

The sub-laminate model with shock EoS was applied to the aluminum sphere hypervelocity impact series and 20 mm FSP ballistic impact series presented in Figure 10, the results of which are shown in Figure 11.

The sub-laminate model is shown to provide a significant improvement in predicting the experimental V_{50} of 394 m/s for the FSP ballistic impacts (377 m/s) compared to the monolithic model (236 m/s).

The ballistic limit and residual velocity predicted with the sub-laminate model for the hypervelocity impact case are shown to be comparable with the original monolithic model. For conditions closer to the ballistic limit, the sub-laminate model is shown to predict increased target resistance (i.e., lower residual velocity). For higher overmatch conditions, there is some small variance between the two approaches.

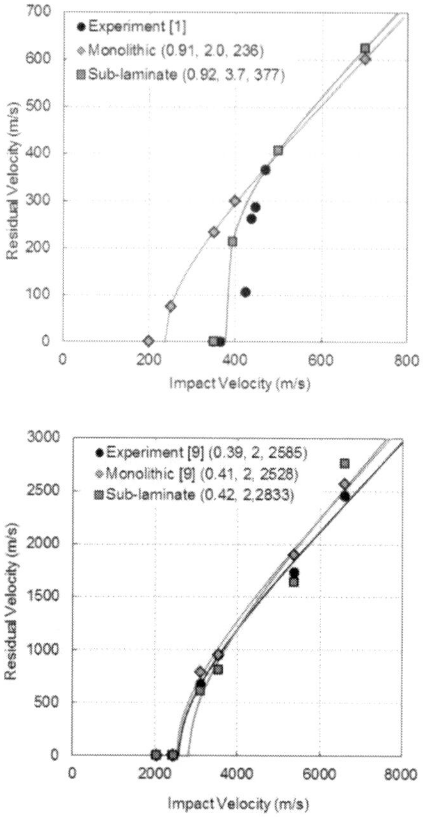

Figure 11. Experimental and numerical results with the two numerical models for 20 mm FSP against 10 mm thick HB26 (above), and 6 mm diameter aluminium spheres against HB26 (below) at normal incidence.

Now, regarding common handgun projectiles, the results look sobering. As the most widespread weapon in the world, the Kalashnikov rifle (AK-47) is a good example to compare ballistic trials and simulation results. A 7.62x39 mm full metal jacket (FMJ) projectile with a velocity of 700 m/s is used and the model is shown in Figure 3.

In Figure 12, a qualitative assessment of the bulge formation is made for the 11 mm panel. Prediction of bulge development is important as it is characteristic of the material wave speed and is also a key measure in defence applications, particularly in personal armour systems (i.e., vests and helmets). In the ballistic experiments, the 11 mm target panel resists the 7.62x39 mm FMJ projectile. On the left, the "state-of-the-art" models of Lässig and Nguyen are shown. But in both models, material fails, and the projectile penetrates the plate.

There is no accurate reproduction of the bulge. The problem is a neglect of micro-structures. Fraction and fragmentation between the laminate layers cannot be described by homogeneous continuum models.

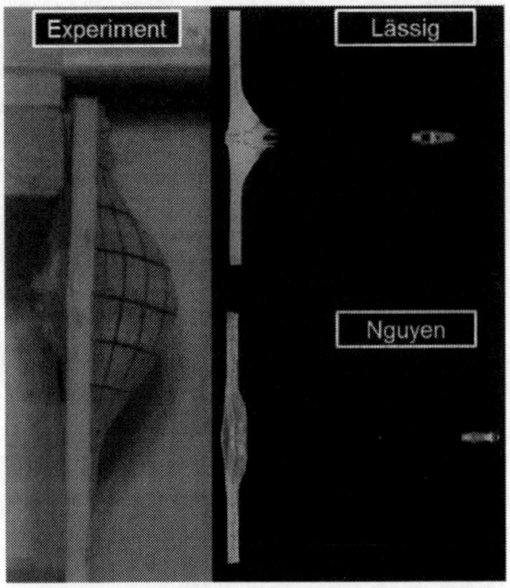

Figure 12. Bulge of a 11 mm target impact by a 7.62×39 mm FMJ projectile at 689 m/s (experiment, left) and the simulation results.

The significant decrease in accuracy of the numerical prediction may be due to an insufficient in-plane tensile strength defined in the material data set, a critical material property in the ballistic performance of fiber reinforced composites. Numerous researchers have investigated the tension properties of UHMW-PE composite (e.g. [6] and [34]). These tests showed that due the low friction coefficient and poor fibre/matrix adhesion in UHMW-PE composites, specimen griping is problematic, often leading to delamination rather than tension failure [8]. These disadvantages are addressed in a very new and more representative model.

VII. Numerical Simulation

As mentioned before, the ballistic tests are followed by computational modelling of the experimental set-up. Then, the experiment is reproduced using numerical simulations. The geometry and observed response of the laminate to ballistic impact is approximately symmetric to the axis through the bullet impact point.

Numerical simulation of modern armor structures requires the selection of appropriate material models for the constituent materials and the derivation of suitable material model input data. The laminate system studied here is an ultra-high molecular weight polyethylene composite. Lead and copper are also required for the projectiles.

A. Geometry

The projectile is a 7.62×39 mm round, a rimless bottlenecked intermediate cartridge of Soviet origin that was designed during World War II. It was divided into different parts - the jacket and the base - which have different properties and even different meshes. These elements have quadratic shape functions and nodes between the element edges. In this way, the computational accuracy, as well as the quality of curved model shapes increases. Using the same mesh density, the application of parabolic elements leads to a higher accuracy compared to linear elements (1st order elements). The standard model geometry was replicated from previous works with targets sized 250×250 mm at thicknesses of 5.5 mm, 11 mm and 16.2 mm.

B. Modelling

Because of the discrepancies discussed in Section VI, a new model was developed – a concept for the numerical simulation of fiber-reinforced plastics under impact loading. Here, the homogeneous continuum model is replaced. Alternating layers of fibers and matrix are used for the geometry. The mesh applied used a central bias to ensure the elements in vicinity of the point of impact were cubic whilst decreasing the overall computational complexity and hence run-time of the simulations. A 0.1 mm gap was placed between each layer for the use of an external gap contact algorithm. It was established in previous works that gapless contacts resulted in overpenetration of elements leading to poorer predictions [1]. An example of the standard model geometry and mesh can be seen in Figure 13.

The fiber layers apply anisotropic elasticity, no plasticity and anisotropic material failure (stress-dependent). The matrix layers use isotropic elasticity, von Mises plasticity and isotropic material failure (stress-dependent). To simulate the effect of delamination, principal stress failure is applied.

3D numerical simulations were performed of the full target and projectile, where both were meshed using 8-node hexahedral elements. The projectile was meshed with 9 elements across the diameter.

The target is composed of sub-laminates that are one element thick, separated by a small gap to satisfy the master-slave contact algorithm (external gap in AUTODYN) and bonded together as previously discussed. The mesh size of the target is approximately equal to the projectile at the impact site. The mesh was then graded towards the edge, increasing in coarseness to reduce the computational load of the model. Since UHMW-PE composite has a very low coefficient of friction, force fit clamping provides little restraint. High speed video of ballistic impact tests typical showed clamp slippage upon impact. As such no boundary conditions were imposed on the target.

C. Thermal Softening

In order to create automatic thermal softening in the UHMW-PE model, a custom subroutine was required that could update the material parameters of each cell based on the local element temperature. The software packages Microsoft Visual Studio 2010 and Intel Professional Fortran Compiler 2013 were used to create the custom subroutines and compile them into AUTODYN® executables. These software packages enabled the implementation of the existing erosion model along with the creation of a new subroutine for the application of thermal softening. The initial standard model was modified as to ensure each sub-laminate layer was defined as a unique material. By this method the subroutine could be called at the end of each cycle to iterate through each sub-laminate layer and modify the material parameters based on the maximum temperature within each layer.

Figure 13. Geometry of a target plate: alternating layers of fibers and matrix are used in the computer model.

In this work, the Young's modulus was not softened since in AUTODYN® it is intimately linked to the equation-of-state and was unlikely to affect the ballistic performance of the laminate. Instead, the master effective stress, plastic strain curve was softened according to the data given by Dessain et al. [35] where a linear decrease in strength was interpolated. Given that softening occurred over the whole individual layer in the laminates as opposed to local cells, it was necessary to introduce a thermal-softening limit. In this work, this limit was set to 50%. The variables that were thermally softened in the model are shown in Table I.

D. Simulation Results

The model developed in [19] was adjusted and the concept has been extended to different calibers and projectile velocities. Composite armor plates between 5.5 and 16.2 mm were tested in several ballistic trials and high-speed videos were used to analyze the characteristics of the projectile – before and after the impact. An example of the simulation results with the modified model and a 7.62×39 mm bullet is shown in Figure 14.

The deformation of the projectile is in good agreement with the experimental observation. Both delamination and fragmentation can be seen in the numerical simulation. Compared to the homogeneous continuum model, fractures can be detected easily. Subsequently, the results of experiment and simulation in the case of perforation were compared with reference to the projectile residual velocity. Here, only minor differences were observed. The results are summarized in Table II.

TABLE I. PARAMETERS THAT WERE CHANGED IN EACH INDIVIDUAL LAYER DUE TO THERMAL SOFTENING

Parameter	Description	Initial value
k	Master effective stress – effective plastic strain curve	-
A22	Plasticity constant, 22	6×10^{-4}
A33	Plasticity constant, 33	6×10^{-4}
S22	Tensile failure stress, 22	1.15 GPa
S33	Tensile failure stress, 33	1.15 GPa

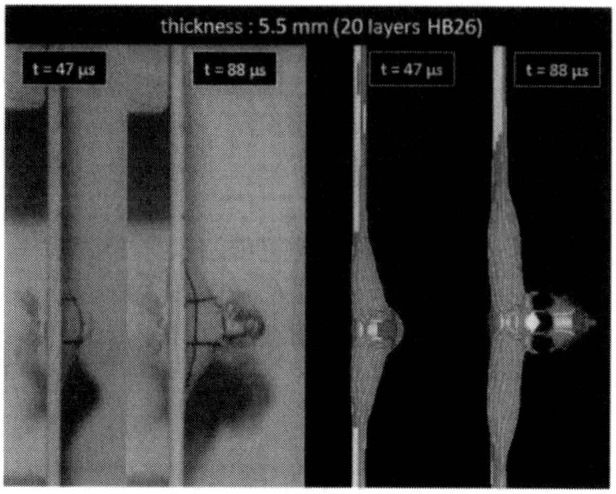

Figure 14. Effect of a 5.5 mm target impact by a 7.62×39 mm bullet at 686 m/s, 47 µs and 88 µs after the initial impact; comparing experimantal (left) and simulation (right) results.

TABLE II. SUMMARY OF RESULTS FOR A 7.62×39 MM BULLET

Target Thickness	5.5 mm Residual Velocity	11.0 mm Residual Thickness	16.2 mm Residual Thickness
Experiment	604 m/s	6 mm	11 mm
Simulation	587 m/s	4 mm	10 mm

It was found that the ballistic limit was satisfactorily reproduced in all cases. The tests showed that the projectile was stopped using thick target panels. Here, the residual thickness was correctly predicted by the FE-simulation.

VIII. CONCLUSION

The material model developed in [19] has some shortcomings regarding the simulation of handgun projectiles (e.g., 7.62×39 mm). Although previously found to provide accurate results for hypervelocity impact of aluminum spheres, the existing model and dataset was found to significantly underestimate the composite performance under impact conditions driven by through-thickness shear performance (ballistic impact of fragment simulating projectiles). The model was found to exhibit premature through thickness shear failure as a result of directional coupling in the modified Hashin-Tsai failure criterion and the large discrepancy between through-thickness tensile and shear strength of UHME-PE composite. As a result, premature damage and failure was initiated in the through-thickness shear direction leading to decreased ballistic performance. By de-coupling through-thickness tensile failure from the failure criteria and discretizing the laminate into a nominal number of kinematically joined sub-laminates through the thickness, progresses in modelling the ballistic response of the panels was improved.

Thermal softening and melting effects have been shown in previous work to account for a large degree of error in the prediction of thick UHMW-PE composite ballistic limit velocities. Through the modification of a custom subroutine the thermal softening effects of UHMW-PE have been adequately modelled in a manner that both saves computational processing time and increases predictive capability through softening whole individual discrete layers of the laminate.

New approaches make it possible to increase the accuracy of the simulation results. The previous concept was not valid for all projectiles/calibers. An alternative model has been developed to overcome these difficulties. Using sub-laminates and inhomogeneities on the macroscale, the model does not match the real microstructure, but allow a more realistic description of the failure processes mentioned above. The numerical model proposed a sub-laminate discretisation of the laminate in order to better model delamination failure. For this to occur, the sub-laminates are joined together using bonded contacts where failure is initiated based on a combined normal and shear stress criterion.

This work also demonstrated how a small number of well-defined experiments can be used to develop, calibrate, and validate solver technologies used for simulating the impact of projectiles on complex armor systems and composite laminate structures. Ballistic trials can be used as the basis of an iterative optimization process. Numerical simulations are a valuable adjunct to the study of the behavior of metals subjected to high-velocity impact or intense impulsive loading. The combined use of computations, experiments and high-strain-rate material characterization has, in many cases, supplemented the data achievable by experiments alone at considerable savings in both cost and engineering man-hours.

REFERENCES

[1] A. Ramezani and H. Rothe, "A New Approach to Modelling Fiber-Reinforced Plastics for Hydrocode Analysis - Experimental Model Validation of Composite Materials Under Ballistic Impact," The Ninth International Conference on Advances in System Simulation (SIMUL 2017) IARIA, Oct. 2017, pp. 41-50, ISBN 978-1-61208-594-4.

[2] R&G Composite Technology, Manual of Fibre Reinforcements. D-71111 Waldenbuch, 2009.

[3] J. Van Dingenen, "Gel-spun high-performance polyethylene fibres," in High Performance Fibres, pp. 62–92, 2001.

[4] B. Russell, K. Karthikeyan, V. Deshpande, and N. Fleck, "The high strain rate response of ultra-high molecular-weight polyethylene: From fibre to laminate," in International Journal of Impact Engineering (60), pp. 1–9, 2013.

[5] L. H. Nguyen, The Ballistic Performance of Thick Ultra High Molecular Weight Polyethylene Composite. RMIT University, 2015.

[6] P. M. Cunniff, "Dimensionless parameters for optimization of textile based body armor systems," in 18th International Symposium on Ballistics, pp. 1303–1310, 1999.

[7] D. B. Segala and P. V. Cavallaro, "Numerical investigation of energy absorption mechanisms in unidirectional composites subjected to dynamic loading events," in Computational Materials Science 81, pp. 303–312, 2014.

[8] S. Chocron et al., "Modeling unidirectional composites by bundling fibers into strips with experimental determination of shear and compression properties at high pressures," in Composites Science and Technology 101, pp. 32–40, 2014.

[9] C. J. Hayhurst, S. J. Hiermaier, R. A. Clegg, W. Riedel, and M. Lambert, "Development of material models for nextel and kevlar-expoxy for high pressures and strain rates," in International Journal of Impact Engineering 23, pp. 365–376, 1999.

[10] R. A. Clegg, D. M. White, W. Riedel, and W. Harwick, "Hypervelocity impact damage prediction in composites: Part I—material model and characterisation," in International Journal of Impact Engineering 33, pp. 190–200, 2006.

[11] W. Riedel, H. Nahme, D. M. White, and R. A. Clegg, "Hypervelocity impact damage prediction in composites: Part II—experimental investigations and simulations," in International Journal of Impact Engineering 33, pp. 670–80, 2006.

[12] M. Wicklein, S. Ryan, D. M. White, and R. A. Clegg, "Hypervelocity impact on CFRP: Testing, material modelling, and numerical simulation," in International Journal of Impact Engineering 35, pp.1861–1869, 2008.

[13] ANSYS. *AUTODYN Composite Modelling Release 15.0.* [Online]. Available from: http://ansys.com/ 2018.07.28.

[14] T. Lässig et al., "A non-linear orthotropic hydrocode model for ultra-high molecular weight polyethylene in impact simulations," in International Journal of Impact Engineering 75, pp. 110–122, 2015.

[15] C. J. Hayhurst, J. Leahy, J., M. van der Jagt-Deutekom, and P. Kelly, "Development of Material Models for Numerical Simulation of Ballistic Impact onto Polyethylene Fibrous Armour," in Personal Armour Systems Symposium, pp. 5–8, 2000.

[16] K. Herlaar, M. van der Jagt-Deutekom, and M. Jacobs, "Finite element simulations and experiments of ballistic impacts on high performance PE composite material," in 22nd International Symposium on Ballistics, pp. 1040–1047, 2005.

[17] C. Ong, C. Boey, R. S. Hixson, and J. O. Sinibaldi, "Advanced layered personnel armor," in International Journal of Impact Engineering 38(5), pp. 369–383, 2011.

[18] U. Heisserer and H. Van der Werff, "The relation between Dyneema fiber properties and ballistic protection performance of its fiber composites," in 15th International Conference on Deformation, Yield and Fracture of Polymers 3, pp. 242–246, 2012.

[19] L. H. Nguyen et al., "Numerical Modelling of Ultra-High Molecular Weight Polyethylene Composite Under Impact Loading," in Procedia Engineering 103, pp. 436–443, 2015.

[20] J. Zukas, Introduction to hydrocodes. Elsevier Science, 2004.

[21] G.-S. Collins, An Introduction to Hydrocode Modeling. Applied Modelling and Computation Group, Imperial College London, 2002.

[22] E. Madenci and I. Guven, "The Finite Element Method and Applications in Engineering Using ANSYS," Springer Verlag, February 2015.

[23] H.-B. Woyand, FEM with CATIA V5. J. Schlembach Fachverlag, 2007.

[24] S. J. Hiermaier, Structures Under Crash and Impact. Spinger Verlag, 2008.

[25] R. F. Stellingwerf and C. A. Wingate, "Impact Modeling with Smooth Particle Hydrodynamics," International Journal of Impact Engineering, vol. 14, pp. 707–718, Sep. 1993.

[26] X. Quan, N. K. Birnbaum, M. S. Cowler, and B. I. Gerber, "Numerical Simulations of Structural Deformation under

Shock and Impact Loads using a Coupled Multi-Solver Approach," 5th Asia-Pacific Conference on Shock and Impact Loads on Structures, Hunan, China, Nov. 2003, pp. 152-161.

[27] ANSYS Inc. Available Solution Methods. [Online]. Available from: http://www.ansys.com/Products/Simulation+Technology/Structural+Analysis/Explicit+Dynamics/Features/Available+Solution+Methods [retrieved: August, 2018]

[28] P. Fröhlich, FEM Application Basics. Vieweg Verlag, September 2005.

[29] J. Zukas, T. Nicholas, H.F. Swift, L. B. Greszczuk, and D. R. Curran, Impact Dynamics, Krieger Publishing, FL: Malabar, 1992.

[30] D. E. Carlucci and S. S. Jacobson, Ballistics: Theory and Design of Guns and Ammunition, CRC Press, FL: Boca Raton, 2007.

[31] OEG Optical Measuring and Test Equipment. [Online]. Available from: http://www.oeg-messtechnik.de/?p=5&l=1 [retrieved: August, 2018]

[32] G. Johnson and W. Cook, "A constitutive model and data for metals subjected to large strains, high strain rates and high temperatures," in 7th International Symposium on Ballistics, pp. 541–547, 1983.

[33] D. Steinberg, Equation of state and strength properties of selected materials. California, 1996.

[34] A. Levi-Sasson, I. Meshi, S. Mustacchi, I. Amarilio, D. Benes, V. Favorsky, R. Eliasy, J. Aboudi, R. Haj-Ali, "Experimental determination of linear and nonlinear mechanical properties of laminated soft composite material system," Composites Part B: Engineering 57, pp. 96–104, 2014.

[35] B. Dessain, O. Moulaert, R. Keunings, and A. R. Bunsell, "Solid Phase Change Controlling the Tensile and Creep Behaviour of Gel- Spun High-Modulus Polyethylene Fibres," in Journal of Material Science, 27 (16), pp. 4515–4522, 1992.

Utilizing Timber Harvest Simulation as a Tool for Education

Daniel Losch and Jürgen Roßmann

Institute for Man-Machine Interaction
RWTH Aachen University
Ahornstr. 55, 52074 Aachen, Germany
Email: {losch, rossmann}@mmi.rwth-aachen.de

***Abstract*—Forestry is an important economic field in Germany as well as world wide. In Germany, specially trained forest managers are in charge of silviculture and preservation of forests. An important part of a forest manager's training is the ability to estimate the economical feasibility and ecological impact of timber harvesting operations. In this contribution, we present timber harvest simulation as a tool to enable teachers to better present these estimations in the forestry classroom. We present the simulation as a featured application of the Forest Management System ClusterWIS, including the developments required to implement our educative approach.**

Keywords–Simulation; Geo Information Systems; Forest Information Systems; Education; Timber Industry.

I. Introduction

An important part of a prospective forest manager's training is economical and ecological planning and calculation of timber harvesting operations. This training is usually done with elementary teaching methods and does not utilize modern, technology-assisted teaching methods. Common calculation methods taught to aspiring forest managers include calculations following official forestry guidelines (e.g,. those of the German state of North-Rhine Westphalia [1]). These guidelines are primarily based on experience, and utilizing them requires only basic knowledge about the areas affected by a harvesting operation.

The usage of limited information is not without drawbacks: It is rarely possible to accurately calculate concrete costs and revenue for a single, custom harvesting operation. The amount of flexibility regarding key process parameters is very limited. Forestry instructors, however, need tools that are more flexible to teach students the influence of different parameters on the outcome of a harvesting operation, and that are customized to the forestry areas used to educate their trainees on site.

Some researchers already approached this problem: Asikainen [2], Bruchner [3], Ziesak et al. [4] and Hemm et al. [5] used simulation to estimate costs and revenues for harvesting operations. However, their approaches were largely limited to a small set of predefined geographic locations, and were still not very flexible regarding different process parameters (e.g., they could only simulate a single mechanized harvester and forwarder). Therefore, we already developed a hybrid discrete-event and quasi-continuous timber harvest simulation system presented in [6] as a more flexible alternative. It offers a grater flexibility than the classical, table-based approaches or the other simulative approaches. It is able to calculate the economical results of a timber harvest operation, and also offers methods to estimate the ecological impact of those operations.

Hence, we propose our simulation system as the basis for a simulation tool that is fit to be used in education. However, it still does not quite offer the required flexibility. With the integration of our simulation system into ClusterWIS, we were able to extend and adapt the system to meet the requirements of educative use, and were even able to improve its' usability for non-simulation experts. In this contribution, we present our extensions and adaptations in detail.

Even so, a flexible simulation system alone is of limited use to forestry trainers. They also need an didactic concept that is adapted for use with the simulation. Teachers need to properly utilize simulation results in their classes to gain all benefits of such a system. Therefore, we also developed such a concept and present it in this contribution.

The structure of this article is as follows: The next section introduces ClusterWIS as as the underlying infrastructure for our approach. Section III presents the ClusterWIS timber harvest simulation system as well as our novel approaches to extend that simulation system and improve its flexibility and usability. Finally, section IV describes a didactic concept for forest manager trainees based on timber harvest simulation in ClusterWIS.

II. The Geo and Forest Information System ClusterWIS

ClusterWIS [7] is a decentralized infrastructure for Geo and Forest Information Systems that originated from the "nD Forest Management System Virtual Forest" [8], [9]. It is implemented using the simulation system VEROSIM® and allows us to readily access several data sources that originated in the Virtual Forest and to develop custom algorithms to process their data for a wide range of applications.

In particular, the following data sources are relevant to timber harvesting and are used by the timber harvesting simulation that is the basis for our didactic concept.

- A land registry that defines forestry sites.
- A high-resolution terrain elevation database (including hill shades).
- A map of forest roads and streets.
- A tree database containing information about location, type, age, and height of trees present in the forestry sites; Because of cost concerns, the entries of this database were not generated by exhaustive forest assessment, but were generated from aerial

Figure 1. 3D view of a simulated mechanized harvester in ClusterWIS.

measurements of tree heights in combination with a pre-existing tree type map, utilizing the methods described in [10].

- A database of forest machinery available for harvest operations.

In addition, ClusterWIS offers the possibility to render clear two-dimensional views of the aforementioned data sources, as well as three-dimensional renderings that intuitively illustrate the nature of the displayed forest areas. Figure 1 displays a simulated mechanized harvester in ClusterWIS. Finally, the service-oriented, distributed nature of the ClusterWIS infrastructure allows for the easy deployment of the simulation system to educational institutions by offering simulation as a service.

III. A CLUSTERWIS-BASED SIMULATION SYSTEM FOR TIMBER HARVESTING OPERATIONS

One of the features that is available in ClusterWIS is a Petri-net based scripting Interface called State Oriented Modelling Language++ [11], [12]. This interface has already been used to prototypically develop a combined discrete-event and quasi-continuous simulation system for timber harvesting in the Virtual Forest [6], [13]. It offers the possibility to simulate and analyse work processes in the field of fully mechanized timber harvesting conducted by harvesters and forwarders. A simulation pass in this system is conducted by completing the following tasks:

1) Select the affected area. This includes an automated import of the forest and skidding roads – also known as logging roads or logging trails – that are used for navigation by mechanized harvest resources.
2) Mark trees in the affected area for felling.
3) Calculate the marked trees' assortments. This includes the process of subdividing felled trees into segments (called *sorts*), usually to optimize the revenue of a felling operation. The relevant parameters in timber assortment are the minimum allowed top diameter of the resulting sorts, and optionally, their lengths.
4) Select harvest resources (i.e., mechanized harvesters and forwarders)
5) Execute the simulation.
6) Review the simulation results.

The behaviour of harvest resources modelled as a multi-agent system by hierarchical, synchronized and timed Petri-net state machines. The synchronized Petri-net components represent the discrete-event portion of the behavioural model and react to events, such as the felling of a tree or the successful unloading of logs at a road. The timed Petri-net components model the quasi-continuous potion of the behaviour and simulate real-time navigation used to determine the position of interacting harvest resources to allow for safety checks (e.g., when a tree is felled by a harvester, all other harvesters have to be at a minimum safety distance). The Petri-nets are executed by the SOML++ scripting interface and interact with the underlying geo information system to execute the models and lead to a simulation of harvesting operations. More details of this simulation approach and the underlying framework can be found in [6].

However, the simulation system included in ClusterWIS is limited with regard to the flexibility of supported process parameters: It only supports simulations of fully mechanized timber harvesting operations and offers a very limited way to calculate timber assortments. It is also confined to a pre-existing database of forest and skidding roads. Those limitations are severe: The definition of assortments is the most important factor in determining the yield and financial revenue of a harvesting operations, and different skidding road spacings may require manual felling of trees, which is an important cost factor.

While discussing our initial concepts for digital timber harvesting education with representatives of a local forestry teaching facility, we realized that we needed to extend the ClusterWIS timber harvest simulation system and add features that address the mentioned shortfalls. The following subsections discuss these adaptations and extensions in detail.

A. *Definition of Custom Skidding Roads*

The positioning – and particularly the distance – between adjacent skidding roads is an important factor for the total work, and correspondingly costs, associated with a harvest operation. If skidding roads are more than two harvester tool ranges (usually 20 m) apart, some trees are not reachable by mechanized harvesters, and thus cannot be felled by them. Since the German Forest Stewardship Council (FSC) standardizes a skidding road distance of at least 40 m for ecological reasons [14], this happens quite regularly. In order to enable users to adequately simulate and compare harvest operations with different sets of skidding roads, we added a tool to customize the road network accordingly, and utilize the resulting roads in simulation. In particular, we added the possibility to generate equidistant skidding roads in an area based on a single prototype, shown in Figure 2.

B. *Simulation of Manual, Mechanized and Mixed Timber Harvesting*

Trees that are outside the range of mechanized harvesters have to be felled manually by lumberjacks. Lumberjacks are not bound to a road network, but can walk up to any tree and fell it utilizing a chainsaw. However, utilizing manual labour in harvesting operations is more expensive and time-consuming than utilizing mechanized harvesters. To profit from the unlimited range and mobility of lumberjacks as well as the efficiency of mechanized harvest, lumberjacks must fell the trees toward the skidding roads, where mechanized harvesters may pick the felled trees up and process them. This includes

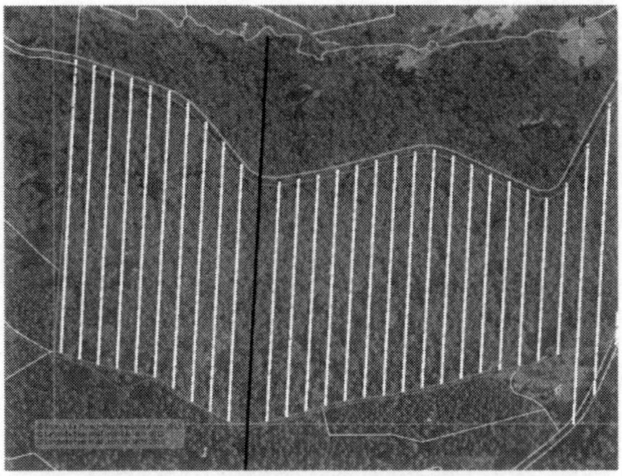

(a) 20 m distance between adjacent skidding roads.

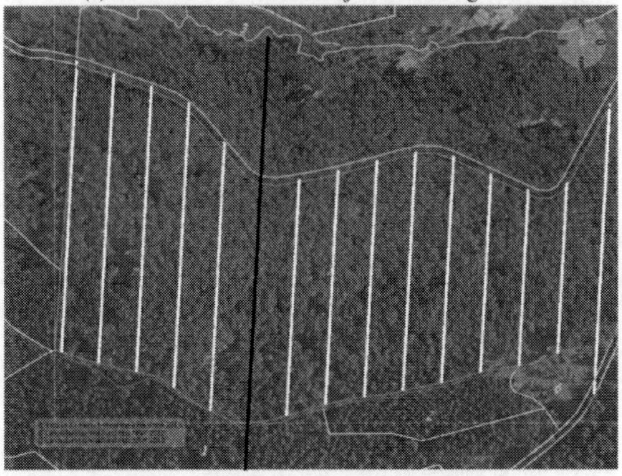

(b) 40 m distance between adjacent skidding roads.

Figure 2. 2D top down view of an exemplary forest area with customized, equidistant skidding roads (white). The black line is the prototypical skidding road used to generate the others.

the de-branching and splitting of the felled trees into sorts. If no harvesters are assigned to a harvest operation, lumberjacks have to conduct the processing as well. Figure 3 shows the simulated behavioural work flow of a lumberjack.

We added the functionality to utilize lumberjacks into our simulation system as a type of harvesting agent by modelling their behaviours as Petri-nets that resemble those nets that model the harvesters' behaviour.

We also added skidders as a new type of harvesting resource. Skidders are manually operated tractors outfitted with tongs or cable winches that can be used to manually transport logs from the wood to the nearest street. In this case, skidders act as the manual counterpart to mechanized wood forwarders. Furthermore, skidders can be used to pull felled trees to skidding roads if they cannot be felled into the harvesters' range.

With the inclusion of manually working harvest resources, the simulation system now offers the following harvest scenarios:

- Fully mechanized harvest with harvesters and forwarders.
- Fully manual harvest with lumberjacks and skidders.

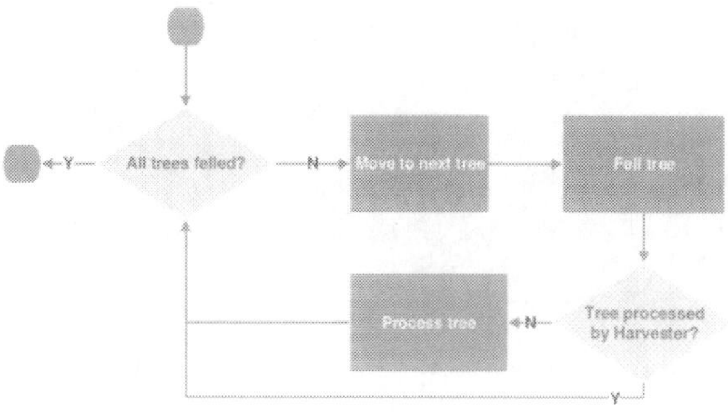

Figure 3. Schematic work flow of a manually harvesting lumberjack.

- Mixed harvest with lumberjacks felling trees that are far away from skidding roads, and harvesters and forwarders conducting all further work steps. Optionally, skidders may be used to pull felled trees toward skidding roads.

C. Improved Interoperability with Timber Assortment Tools

When adding the possibility to simulate lumberjacks, we realized that manual and mechanized harvest utilizes different approaches for timber assortment: While mechanized harvesters predominantly produce fixed-length log segments, the process of repeated manual bucking by lumberjacks is quite labour-intensive and therefore expensive. Consequently, manual harvest is usually used to fell whole logs. However, the pre-existing interface from the simulation system to the timber assortment tool BDAT [15] could only execute fixed-length sortimentation. We extended this interface to support the calculation of whole-log sortimentations. We also added the commonly used parameter of minimum top diameter to the interface. This parameter defines a minimum diameter for each harvested log or log segment. Smaller segments are regarded as industrial-grade wood and are valued less.

After discussions with domain experts, we realized that BDAT, while enabling a fast and easy-to-configure calculation of assortments, lacks flexibility that is desired in practice. Therefore, we decided to add a new interface to the HOLZERNTE (German for "timber harvesting") software package [16] that is developed at the Forest Research Institute Baden-Württemberg and allows for arbitrary, highly customized assortments. However, this software is only used with an extensive forestry background and lacks performance when calculating sorts. To overcome the second limitation, our software interface generates a limited number of representative, virtual trees that are sorted by HOLZERNTE. The resulting assortments are re-used for multiple trees that are most similar to the respective virtual one.

With the extension of the BDAT interface and the addition of the HOLZERNTE interface, users are now able to choose between two easy to use and fast, yet simple methods to calculate assortments and one that is highly flexible, but more difficult to use.

D. Support For Wood Quality Classes in Revenue Calculation

Wood prices—and therefore the potential revenue from a completed timber harvest operation—are dependent not only

Results

During this harvest operation, 407 trees with an average diameter breast height of 28,44 cm were felled. A total volume of 261,21 m³ was harvested.

Revenue and Costs

Calculation	Amount Value (€)	Wood Volume (m³)	Amount Value per Wood Volume (€/m³)
Lumberjack	204,51		
Lumberjack	160,66		
Lumberjack	167,60		
Harvester	2 375,69		
Forwarder	1 683,00		
Total Costs for Felling and Processing	2 908,48	261,21	11,13
Total Costs for Skidding	1 683,00	261,21	6,44
Total Costs	4 591,48	261,21	17,58
Gross Revenue	19 953,95	261,21	76,39
Net Revenue	15 362,47	261,21	58,81
Lost Revenue	206,60	2,85	72,42

Figure 4. Screen shot of economic results generated by a simulation run, as displayed in our custom HTML template (translated to English).

on the previously mentioned assortment, but also on the quality of the wood itself. In Germany, wood quality is measured in quality classes, which abstract from quality factors as irregular growth, cracks or insect damage [17]. Since we were able to obtain wood price tables that are differentiated into these quality classes, we added the possibility to assign quality classes to the harvested assortments to the BDAT interface, and to extract the corresponding data from the calculation results of the HOLZERNTE software.

With these changes, users can choose to set the harvested woods' quality and calculate felling revenues dependant on this parameter, regardless of the chosen assortment algorithm.

E. Analysis and Presentation of Simulation Results

During discussions with domain experts, we realized that we needed to rework the results statistics previously displayed by the simulation system: The statistics were incomplete, unclear, and displaying them on high-resolution and high-DPI monitors was not possible. Therefore, we completely replaced the statistics display of the ClusterWIS wood harvest simulation system. In order to reach compatibility with arbitrary display sizes and resolutions, we designed a HTML-based template as the foundation for our results display, thereby shifting the responsibility for correct rendering of our results to the web browser used to display them.

The first part of our results page (see Figure 4) displays the economical outcome of an exemplary simulation run of a mixed harvest scenario that does not utilize skidders. The economical outcome table contains a breakdown of all simulated felling costs and the expected total revenue of the harvested logs. It also contains a row displaying potential revenue that was lost, because not all trees could be felled due to their distance to the skidding roads.

Our results page also contains a set of detailed statistics tables of all harvested sorts (grouped by tree type and sort class and sort quality class) and their corresponding values. For comparison, we also display a similar table for all assortments that could not be harvested (e.g., because they were out of range of the harvesters in a fully mechanized harvesting operation).

Harvester

Work Breakdown:

Action	Time (total)	Time (per Wood Volume)
Driving	01:21:19	00:00:19
Positioning	01:38:42	00:00:23
Felling	00:59:44	00:00:14
Processing	07:11:10	00:01:39
Total (RAZ)	11:10:54	00:02:34
Total (MAS)	13:25:05	00:03:05
Total (GAZ)	16:06:06	00:03:42

Statistics:

Criterium	Value	
Felled Trees	231	
Processed Trees	407	
Processed Wood Volume	261,21 m³	
Efficiency	16,22 m³/h	
Distance Driven	5 212,79 m	19,96 m/m³
Fuel Consumption	187,65 l	0,72 l/m³
Average Driving Speed	3,85 km/h	
Houly Costs (including Fuel)	177,05 €/MAS	

*

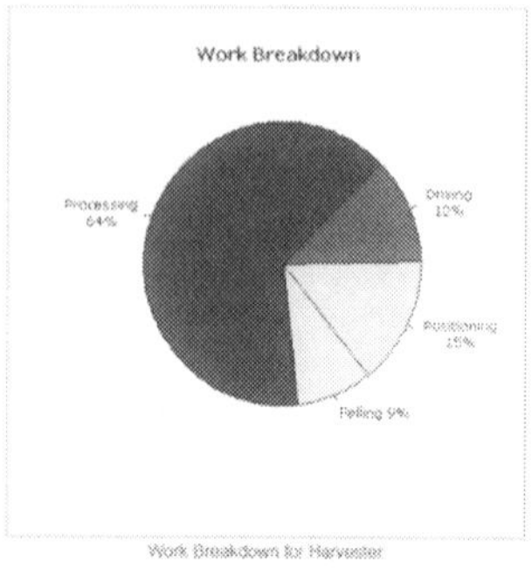

Figure 5. Screenshot of work statistics calculated from a simulation run, as displayed in our custom HTML template (translated to English).

Results Comparison

Comparing results for a table-based calculation and a simulation-based calculation.

Results Overview

Name	Harvested Trees	Wood Volume (m³)	Gross Revenue (€)	Total Costs (€)	Net Revenue (€)
Table-Based Calculation	Ø	108,90	8.875,35	3.913,87	4.961,48
Simulation-Based Calculation	130	128,75	10.857,78	3.834,06	7.023,73

Figure 6. Screen shot of an exemplary results comparison table (translated to English).

The last part of our results page consists of work statistics tables for each simulated harvest resource. These tables show the allocation of work time to the different work steps (e.g., driving, felling, debranching or log loading), and some efficiency statistics such as total fuel consumption and work efficiency (i.e., harvested wood volume per hour). We also added a pie chart to offer a quick overview of the work time allocation for each resource. Figure 5 shows an exemplary statistics table. For forwarders, the statistics include a calculation of the minimum, maximum, and average forwarding distance. These statistics are similar to the statistics generated in the former version of the simulation system, and are not described in detail.

In order to be able to compare different harvesting scenarios, we also added a HTML template that combines the economical results of multiple harvest operations. That template can be used to navigate to the previously described in-depth simulation statistics. An example is given in Figure 6. The felling names are links to detailed result pages containing the information described above. The table-based approach (as described in [1]) is not able to calculate a number of harvested trees, since this approach is solely based on wood volume.

IV. Educational Use of Timber Harvesting Simulation

We propose the use of timber harvesting simulation with an interactive, discussion-based didactic approach. Depending on the availability of simulation system instances in the classroom, there are different ways to integrate our extended simulation system into such a concept.

If there is only one simulation system instance available, teachers may want to discuss the relevant simulation parameters (as described in Sections III and III) with their students and display simulation results on a frontal display. The selection of parameters can be done in form of a interactive discussion based on the information displayed by the Geo Information System components of our simulation system. When focussing on a specific aspect of timber harvesting, teachers can set up different simulation runs that differ in only one or two parameters that fit the topic of the lesson. Students can compare the different simulation runs' results to analyse the economical or ecological impact of the changed parameters.

If there are multiple simulation system instances available, students can work in groups to explore the impact of different parameters themselves and try to optimize simulation parameters (selected by the teacher in accordance to the lessons' topic) with regard to financial profit, work efficiency or ecological impact. The students may then present their results to the class and discuss their discoveries.

In both scenarios, teachers may want to restrict the simulation to geographical areas located in the vicinity of the class room. That enables them to take their students to a field trip to that area where the students can try to transfer their simulation-based results to the real world. Teachers can discuss the discrepancies between the (potentially inaccurate, incomplete or out-of-date) data present in the simulation system and the actual area and present restrictions on the simulation parameters that follow from these discrepancies. These restrictions can be taken into consideration when conducting simulation in a later lesson.

When teachers employ our simulation system in their classes as described above, they can deepen their students' knowledge and understanding of the different aspects of timber harvesting. They can focus on any aspect their curriculum requires and can discuss and compare a wide range of possible statistical results that are relevant to real-world use.

A. *Exemplary Lesson Plan*

We present an exemplary lesson plan that focusses on the difference between fully mechanized and mixed harvest (as described in Section III-B). The lesson plan assumes the availability of our simulation system for the teacher only. It requires a fundamental theoretic understanding of the presented topics by the students, and assumes the teacher to be a certified forestry management educator with corresponding background knowledge about timber harvesting processes, and with an introductory training in the simulation system.

1) The students discuss guidelines for skidding road placement in tandem with the teacher. One important guideline to consider is the German FSC that requires a distance of 40 m between skidding roads.
2) The students utilize hill shades maps, aerial photographs and a 3D view of the terrain to develop concrete skidding road placements according to the guidelines. The teacher adds them to the simulation system.
3) The teacher adds a new set of parameters to the timber harvest simulation system.
4) The teacher presents different methods to select trees for felling and utilizes one method to mark trees for felling in the simulation system.
5) The students discuss different possible timber assortments. The teacher adds a corresponding assortment to the simulation parameters.
6) The students develop different possible resource configurations in tandem with the teacher. They discuss each configurations' advantages and disadvantages (e.g., regarding felling costs or tree reachability from the skidding roads).
7) The teacher chooses a fully mechanized harvesting configuration (i.e., one mechanized harvester and one forwarder) and adds it to the parameter set.
8) The teacher starts the simulation. After the simulation is finished, they open the results page.
9) The students analyse the results with the teacher. They are expected to realize that soil stress concentrates on paths leading up to the landing site (Figure 7a) and that some trees are out of range of the harvesters and remain unharvested (Figure 7b).
10) The teacher adds a set of lumberjacks to the simulation parameters and repeats the simulation.
11) The students analyse the new results and compare them with the previous ones. They are expected to realize that more (possibly all) trees were harvested in the second simulation, and accordingly, the gross revenue has increased. The cost per harvested wood volume has gone up due to the utilisation of (relatively expensive) lumberjacks.

During step 2, the students may rely on physical maps of the area, map views offered by the Geo Information System, or a mix of both. Steps 4 and 5 are not in the focus of the presented lesson and should be discussed only briefly. They may be discussed in detail in another lesson.

Another topic that may be presented in a different lesson is the environmental impact of harvest operations. In such a lesson, the teacher may compare soil stress (see Figure 7a) and fuel consumption resulting from the use of smaller/larger forwarders or different (or multiple) landing sites. Such a comparison can be found in [6].

V. Conclusion

In this contribution, we presented extensions and usability improvements to the ClusterWIS-based system for timber harvest simulation. We aimed for the improvement of the users' flexibility when configuring the simulation parameters. In order to do so, we completely reworked the assortment interface and enabled users to utilize a professional external program to finely tune the assortments to their requirements. We also allowed users to create their own skidding road networks and consequently simulate manual felling of trees. We finally replaced the former results display by a navigable, HTML-based results document.

In the end, all these improvements allowed us to develop a concept for educational use of timber harvesting simulations in training forestry managers, included in the decentralized forest information infrastructure ClusterWIS. We presented this didactic concept and illustrated it with a corresponding exemplary lesson plan.

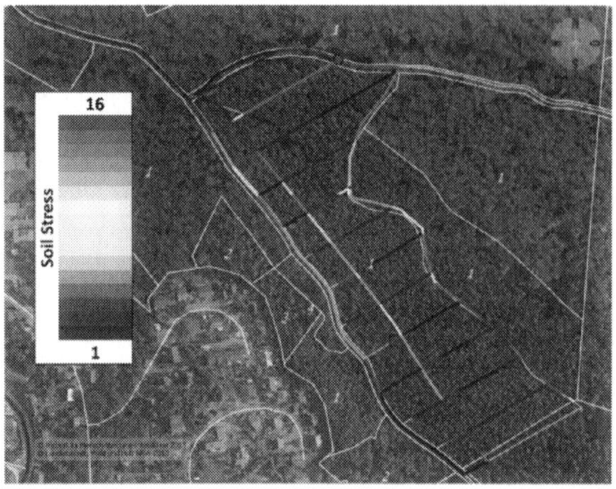

(a) Number of passages of mechanized harvest resources over skidding roads as an indicator of resulting soil stress [18]. Maximum soil stress occurs near the landing site, where all felled logs are collected.

(b) Trees that could not be felled due to their distance to skidding roads are marked red.

Figure 7. Results of a fully mechanized timber harvesting operation with a skidding road distance of 40 m

ACKNOWLEDGEMENT

The authors would like to thank the staff at Forstliches Bildungszentrum Arnsberg for supplying us with revised editions of wood price tables and with realistic machine parameters to utilize in our simulation. The authors would also like to thank Tobias Marquardt and Thomas Gerritzen of RIF e.V. for their help with implementation and testing, and for participating in valuable discussions.

The research project ClusterWIS is co-financed by the European Union and the German federal state of North Rhine-Westphalia: European Union - Investing in our Future - European Regional Development Fund (EFRE-0800088).

REFERENCES

[1] Ministerium für Umwelt und Naturschutz, Landwirtschaft und Verbraucherschutz des Landes Nordrhein-Westfalen, "Richtlinien zur Waldbewertung in Nordrhein-Westfalen [Forest Assessment Guidelines for North-Rhine Westphalia]," 2018.

[2] A. Asikainen, Discrete-event simulation of mechanized wood-harvesting systems. University of Joensuu, 1995.

[3] A.-K. Bruchner, "Industrial simulation software as a decision support tool for harvesting logistics in the wood production chain," Ph.D. dissertation, TU Munich, Germany, 2003.

[4] M. Ziesak, A.-K. Bruchner, and M. Hemm, "Simulation technique for modelling the production chain in forestry," European Journal of Forest Research, vol. 123, no. 3, 2004, pp. 239–244. [Online]. Available: http://dx.doi.org/10.1007/s10342-004-0028-4

[5] M. Hemm, M. Ziesak, and W. Warkotsch, "Simulating harvesting procedures to evaluate different working systems based on discrete single tree events," in Proceedings of the International Precision Forestry Symposium. Citeseer, 2006, pp. 205–220.

[6] D. Losch and J. Roßmann, "Simulation-based analysis of mechanized wood harvest operations," in Industrial Engineering and Applications (ICIEA), 2017 4th International Conference on. IEEE, 2017, pp. 5–9.

[7] J. Rossmann et al., "ClusterWIS - A Decentralized Forest Information and Management System for the Cluster Forestry and Wood," in The Tenth International Conference on Advanced Geographic Information Systems, Applications, and Services (GEOProcessing 2018) IARIA, Rückemann and Doytsher, Eds. IARIA (International Academy, Research, and Industry Association), Mar 2018, pp. 29–35.

[8] J. Roßmann, M. Schluse, A. Bücken, T. Jung, and P. Krahwinkler, "Der virtuelle Wald in NRW [The Virtual Forest in North-Rhine Westphalia," AFZ Der Wald–Allgemeine Forst Zeitschrift für Wald und Forstwirtschaft, vol. 18, 2007, pp. 966–971.

[9] J. Roßmann, M. Schluse, and C. Schlette, "The virtual forest: Robotics and simulation technology as the basis for new approaches to the biological and the technical production in the forest," in Proceedings of the 13th World Multi-Conference Conference on Systems, Cybernetics and Informatics, WMSCI, 2009, pp. 43–48.

[10] J. Rossmann, M. Schluse, A. Bücken, and P. Krahwinkler, "Using airborne laser-scanner-data in forestry management: A novel approach to single tree delineation," in Proceedings of the ISPRS Workshop on Laser Scanning, 2007, pp. 350–354.

[11] J. Roßmann, M. Schluse, and R. Waspe, "Integrating object oriented petri nets into the active graph database of a real time simulation system," in Proceedings of the Winter Simulation Conference. Winter Simulation Conference, 2012, p. 383.

[12] D. Losch, M. Schluse, and J. Roßmann, "Object-Oriented Petri Net-Based Scripting for eRobotics," in 30th European Simulation and Modelling Conference (ESM 2016), Dubai, UAE, 2016.

[13] RIF e.V. et al., "Der Virtuelle Wald – Abschlussbericht [The Virtual Forest – Final Project Report]," Projektkosortium Virtueller Wald III, Tech. Rep., 2014.

[14] E. Seizinger, "German FSC-Standard and Small Forest Standard," Forest Stewardship Council, Arbeitsgruppe Deutschland e.V., Tech. Rep., 2012, URL: https://ic.fsc.org/file-download.fsc-forest-stewardship-standard-for-germany.a-1682.pdf [accessed: 2018-07-31].

[15] E. Kublin and G. Scharnagl, Verfahrens-und Programmbeschreibung zum BWI-Unterprogramm BDAT [Method and Program Description regarding the BWI-Subprogram BDAT]. Forstliche Versuchs-und Forschungsanstalt Baden-Württemberg, 1988.

[16] W. Schoepfer, W. Avemark, and D. Stöhr, "Sorten-, Erlös-und Kostenkalkulation in der Holzernte – eine PC-gestützte Entscheidungshilfe für den Forstbetrieb [Calculation of sorts, revenue and costs – a computer-assisted forestry decision support system]," Forst und Holz, vol. 51, no. 14, 1996, pp. 457–461.

[17] S. Haas, Rahmenvereinbarung für den Rohholzhandel in Deutschland (RVR): vereinbart zwischen dem Deutschen Forstwirtschaftsrat e.V. und dem Deutschen Holzwirtschaftsrat e.V. [General agreement regarding raw timber trade in Germany; negotiated between Deutscher Forstwirtschaftsrat e.V and Deutscher Holzwirtschaftsrat e.V.], ser. ForstBW Praxis. Landesbetrieb ForstBW, 2016.

[18] R. Horn, J. Vossbrink, and S. Becker, "Modern forestry vehicles and their impacts on soil physical properties," Soil and Tillage Research, vol. 79, no. 2, 2004, pp. 207–219.

Sensitivity Analysis of Simulation Study Results on Safety Stock Relaxation in Material Requirement Planning

Sonja Strasser, Klaus Altendorfer, Andreas Peirleitner
Production and Operations Management
University of Applied Sciences Upper Austria
Steyr, Austria
e-mail: {sonja.strasser, klaus.altendorfer, andreas.peirleitner}@fh-steyr.at

Abstract—**In Material Requirement Planning, the lack of capacity constraints can lead to production plans, which cannot be fulfilled on time. One countermeasure for coping with capacity problems is a temporary relaxation of safety stock, which can be implemented in different ways. In this paper, three variants for relaxing safety stock are presented and compared in a simulation study for a simple manufacturing structure. All three methods reveal a significant potential of improvement in comparison to MRP. In a sensitivity analysis, the influence of two MRP planning parameters, i.e., safety stock and production lot size, on the overall costs and the relationship between these two parameters are examined.**

Keywords-Discrete Event Simulation; Sensitivity Analysis; Material Requirements Planning; Safety Stock Relaxation.

I. INTRODUCTION

In production planning, Material Requirement Planning (MRP) [1] is widely applied due to its well comprehensible algorithm for scheduling production orders to satisfy material requirements by external demand. However, there are some weak points of MRP like the assumption of infinite machine capacity and constant production lead times [2] [3]. Neglecting capacity constraints leads to the generation of usually infeasible production plans by MRP, which require additional planning effort at the production control level [4] - [6].

In the last decades, several approaches have been developed to deal with the drawbacks of MRP. Especially for the integration of capacity constraints, there exist a set of different solution approaches [7]. One possibility is to react on capacity problems after the MRP run [4] [5] [8], although it is hard to solve these problems, which are generated at the higher MRP level. Some authors start before the MRP run and try to avoid capacity violations already at the Master Production Schedule (MPS) level [9] [10]. Another approach is the formulation of an optimization problem with capacity constraints instead of the MRP run [11] [12]. In addition to the high computational effort for solving real world planning problems, the theoretical formulations limit the practical application of these approaches. The integration of a solution heuristic into the well-known MRP algorithm for tackling the capacity constraints is another possibility, which is more likely to be accepted for practical implementations. Different approaches can be found in [7], [13]- [16].

In [16], capacity planning is integrated into MRP by providing simple algorithmic measures, like the temporary relaxation of safety stock, load dependent dynamic planned lead times and lot size adaption heuristics. The basic concepts of Material and Capacity Requirements Planning (MCRP) are provided, but details on the implementations are missing. First insights on the performance of the MCRP algorithm are presented in [17] with a simulation study of a simplified production system structure, with eight final products and three Bill Of Material (BOM) levels.

In this paper, two variations of the safety stock relaxation for capacity load balancing, introduced in [16], are defined (Section II) and their performance is compared to the initial implementation and traditional MRP in a simulation study (Section III). To derive a better understanding of the proposed methods for safety stock relaxation, a sensitivity analysis of two MRP planning parameters on the performance of the production system is conducted and the interrelationship of these parameters is investigated in Section IV in detail. In Section V, concluding remarks summarize the main results and outline future research.

II. SAFETY STOCK RELAXATION

A. *Production System*

The modeled production system structure applied in this paper is motivated by different automotive suppliers' production systems and similar to the production system presented in [18]. However, it is a very streamlined version (low number of products, simple BOM structure, only one machine per low level code) to not disturb the simulation experiment results unnecessarily, which are generated later on. Figure 1 shows the resources, bill of material and work schedule applied.

The studied production system is a pure Make-to-Order (MTO) system. Eight final products (low level code, i.e., LLC, 0) are delivered to a set of different customers stating their orders with a random customer required lead time in advance of the respective due date. These final products consist of 1 piece of a semi-processed material on LLC 1 and 2, whereby the raw materials on LLC 3 are assumed to be always available. One machine is available for each processing step and the transformation from one low-level code to the next always includes one processing step. The lot sizing policy is Fixed Order Periods (FOP) for all materials (see [19] for details). The different scenario parameterizations concerning processing times, setup times, demand behavior and customer required lead time are introduced in Section III.

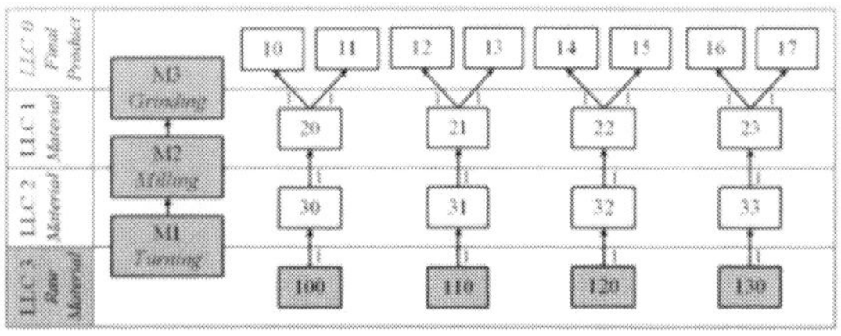

Figure 1. Production System.

B. *Safety Stock Relaxation Method 1*

A safety stock within MRP is applied to reduce the negative effects of uncertainties in customer demand and production processes. From a planning perspective the safety stock is never undershot in the original MRP algorithm (see netting in MRP algorithm, [19] and [1]) and is only used for unplanned occurrences. In the approach introduced in [16], safety stock is already applied in the planning algorithm for capacity load balancing, i.e., available safety stocks are used to temporary reduce the capacity needed. This leads to a shift in capacity consumption since this safety stock has to be refilled in later periods, which leads to a higher capacity consumption there. The basic idea behind that measure is that capacity shortages are only temporary and, therefore, some idle capacity is available further in the future, i.e., capacity load is balanced.

The integration into MRP looks as follows: The MRP algorithm starts with the steps netting and lot sizing for all materials at the respective LLC. After these two steps for all machines at the respective LLC the cumulated capacity needed is calculated. If the cumulated capacity is higher than the available capacity within one planning period, a safety stock relaxation is performed. These three steps (netting, lot sizing and capacitating) are conducted identically for all safety stock relaxation methods evaluated.

In safety stock relaxation method 1, the safety stock for a specific material can only be reduced if there is a planned order receipt in the period of the capacity problem. (Note, that the applied lot sizing rule FOP summarizes net requirements of multiple periods, so there isn't a planned order receipt for each material in every period.) The safety stock is only reduced to the level needed, that the capacity problem in the period of the capacity problem is solved (cumulated capacity needed is equal or smaller than the available capacity). The safety stock is reduced to the end of the coverage of the current FOP lot size. Additionally, a minimum safety stock level can be considered as lower bound. For the application of the safety stock relaxation method, the materials are ordered according to their capacity consumption per piece at the respective machine. The method starts with the material, which has the highest capacity consumption per piece and is performed for further materials until the capacity problem is solved.

The following steps are again performed for all safety stock relaxation methods in the same way. The MRP steps netting and lot sizing are recalculated including the relaxed safety stocks. The MRP algorithm ends with the steps backward scheduling and BOM explosion for all materials at the respective LLC.

C. *Safety Stock Relaxation Method 2*

Safety stock relaxation method 2 starts similar as method 1 with the MRP steps netting and lot sizing and the calculation of the cumulated capacity needed until a capacity problem is detected. In method 1 the safety stock relaxation can only be performed, if there is a planned order receipt in the period of the capacity problem. In method 2, this restriction is removed. A safety stock relaxation can also be performed, if there is a planned order receipt that covers net requirements (due to lot sizing policy FPO) in the period of the capacity problem. This allows that the safety stock for planned order receipts with end dates before the period of the capacity problem can be relaxed. The consequence is that the amount of materials, for which a safety stock relaxation can be performed, is extended. Safety stock relaxation method 2 ends with recalculation of netting, lot sizing, backward scheduling and BOM explosion.

D. *Safety Stock Relaxation Method 3*

Safety stock relaxation method 3 is an extension to method 2 and uses the same logic for the safety stock relaxation. In comparison to method 2, the relaxed safety stock numbers are stored for the next MRP run, usually for the next day. The next MRP run is calculated with the predefined relaxed safety stocks.

Method 3 has the effect that when a safety stock relaxation for a planned order receipt is made, it is never revised. The only exception is that the safety stock can be further relaxed to the minimum safety stock, if there is a new capacity problem. The safety stock is then refilled with future planned order receipts.

III. SIMULATION STUDY

In this section, we outline the design of the simulation study and evaluate the performance of the three different methods for safety stock relaxation, presented in Section II, in comparison to MRP. For the simulation study, the generic simulation framework SimGen based on AnyLogic©, also used in [18], is applied.

A. *Scenario Definition*

To evaluate the performance of the safety stock relaxation method in comparison to MRP, a production system with high work load is selected. If there is a low work load in comparison to the available capacity, methods for capacity balancing would be pointless. Starting with customer demands (log-normally distributed with a coefficient of variation of 1), which result in a shop load of 100% without setup, a scenario with 95% is generated by multiplying the monthly demand with a utilization factor of 95% minus a predefined percentage of setup activities (5% and 10%). A higher percentage setup leads to more time, which is spent for setup. The resulting demand for, e.g., final product 10 with initial demand of 1,059 pcs/month, a utilization factor of 95% and percentage setup of 5%, is 953 pcs/month.

Applicable Customer Required Lead (CRL) time values are estimated in a preliminary simulation study. Summing up the average production lead times for each processing stage delivers a basic lead time value. The average CRL for our simulation study is determined by multiplying this basic lead time value with a CRL factor of 3. To model stochastic effects in CRL a log-normal distribution with a coefficient of variation of 0.5 is applied. In our simulation model, all customer orders are accepted. Due to an average utilization of 95% in the considered production system, short term overloads can be balanced in future periods or by covering customer orders with safety stocks.

Overall costs, consisting of holding and tardiness costs are selected as performance measure. The holding costs per piece and day are 1 CU for final products, 0.5 CU for semi-processed materials and the tardiness costs for final products are 19 CU per piece and day. In the simulation study, 5 years are simulated, where the first year is considered as the warm-up period and therefore excluded from the analysis. Due to the stochastic effects in demand and customer required lead time, each iteration is evaluated with 10 replications.

B. *Planning Parameters*

Applied lot sizing rules, safety stock levels and planned lead times are important planning parameters for MRP [19]. In our simulation study, we choose Fixed Order Period (FOP) as lot sizing policy and the number of periods, for which the demand is accumulated into one production lot, as a planning parameter. To examine the influence of different safety stock levels, a safety stock factor is introduced as planning parameter. The actual safety stock is the initial value of safety stock multiplied with the safety stock factor. The fixed planned lead time of MRP is introduced as a factor, which is multiplied by the basic lead time values. These values are generated in the preliminary study, which is already used for setting customer required lead time values (see Section A. Scenario Definition). The initial value for safety stock of a product type is its average demand per day, i.e., a safety stock factor of 4 means that the average demand of 4 days is kept on safety stock.

For the safety stock relaxation methods, defined in Section II, a lower bound for the safety stock is introduced as an additional planning parameter. This minimum safety stock is again implemented as a factor that is multiplied with the applied safety stock. In order to get reasonable planning parameters for the safety stock relaxation methods, as well as for MRP, a grid search procedure is applied. Table I shows the specified values for all planning parameters.

TABLE I. PARAMETER SETTINGS

Parameter	Values
FOP periods	{4,5,6,8,10,12,14,16}
Safety stock factor	{0,1,2,4,6,8,16}
Planned lead time factor	{0,0.5,1,1.5,2,2.7}
Minimum safety stock factor	{0, 0.25, 0.5, 0.75}

C. *Results of Safety Stock Relaxation and MRP*

Due to different percentages of setup (5%, 10%), two different production scenarios are investigated. For each method of safety stock relaxation and MRP, the parameter combination that leads to minimal overall costs is selected. Table II shows the results for 5% setup. All methods for safety stock relaxation reduce the overall costs significantly, whereby method 3 delivers the best result. The number of FOP periods and the planned lead time factor are similar for all methods, only the safety stock factor is higher for method 2 and 3. In the cost minimum solution, the introduced minimum safety stock factor is only applied for method 3.

TABLE II. OPTIMAL SETTINGS (5% SETUP)

	MRP	Method 1	Method 2	Method 3
Minimum overall costs	10426.6	8319.2	8112.1	7595.7
Relative Improvement	-	-18.1%	-20.2%	-25.3%
FOP periods	6	5	5	5
Safety stock factor	4	4	16	8
Planned lead time factor	1.5	2	1.5	1.5
Minimum safety stock factor	-	0	0	0.25

TABLE III. OPTIMAL SETTINGS (10% SETUP)

	MRP	Method 1	Method 2	Method 3
Minimum overall costs	10163.6	8498.1	9528.0	9760.7
Relative Improvement	-	-16.4%	-6.3%	-4.0%
FOP periods	6	8	6	6
Safety stock factor	6	4	8	8
Planned lead time factor	1	1.5	1	1
Minimum safety stock factor	-	0	0.5	0.5

In the scenario with 10% setup (see Table III), safety stock relaxation is also advantageous in comparison to MRP, whereby in this system with higher setup times, method 1 leads to the best result. The selected parameters show that method 2 and 3 demand for a higher safety stock and a minimum amount of this safety stock, which must not be used for relaxation. Again, FOP periods and planned lead time factors don't reveal major differences for the applied methods. An interesting result concerning the comparison of safety stock relaxation methods is that method 1, i.e., having less safety stock relaxation occurrences but recalculating these each MRP run, leads to similar cost reduction potentials independently of the setup times. However, methods 2 and 3, i.e., allowing the safety stock to be reduced more often, do not perform that well if setup times are high. This might be related to the fact that safety stock reduction sometimes implies a new production lot to refill the safety stock after finishing a lot with reduced safety stocks. The negative impact of this unintended behavior is higher if setup times are higher.

IV. Sensitivity Analysis

In this section, the influence of the two MRP parameters FOP periods and safety stock factor is investigated in a sensitivity analysis to create a comprehensive understanding of how the three introduced methods behave, also in comparison to MRP. The influence on the performance, as well as the interrelationship of these parameters, is analyzed.

A. *The Influence of FOP Periods on Performance*

The application of four different methods and two different percentages of setup lead to eight different cases, which are examined separately. For each specified value of the number of FOP periods (see Table I), we select the combination of the other planning parameters, which results in minimal overall costs. Additionally we also show the amount of inventory and tardiness costs in Figure 2.

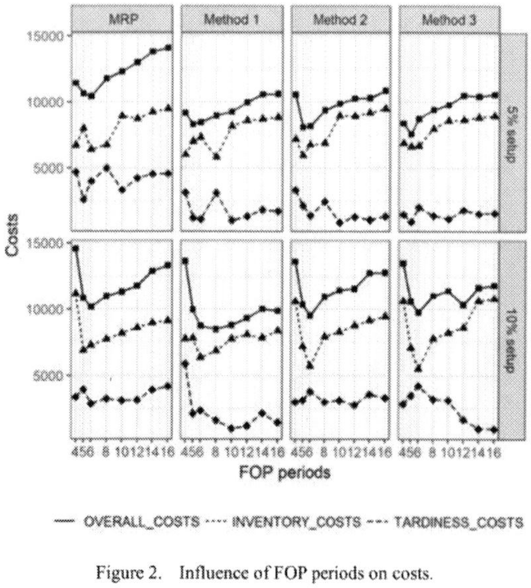

Figure 2. Influence of FOP periods on costs.

All cases show a more or less convex function for overall costs with respect to FOP periods with just a few outliers. As already mentioned in Section III, the optimal value for FOP periods are almost the same for all four methods. A low number of FOP periods leads to significant higher overall costs in the 10% setup scenario, whereas a higher number leads to a moderate increase in costs. For all numbers of FOP periods optimal inventory costs exceed optimal tardiness costs considerably. Apart from some outliers for small number of FOP periods, the inventory costs show a convex behavior with respect to the FOP periods. These results are in line with analytical production system findings without capacity balancing [20].

B. *The Influence of Safety Stock Factor on Performance*

For the safety stock factor, the same analysis as for the FOP periods is performed and the results can be found in Figure 3.

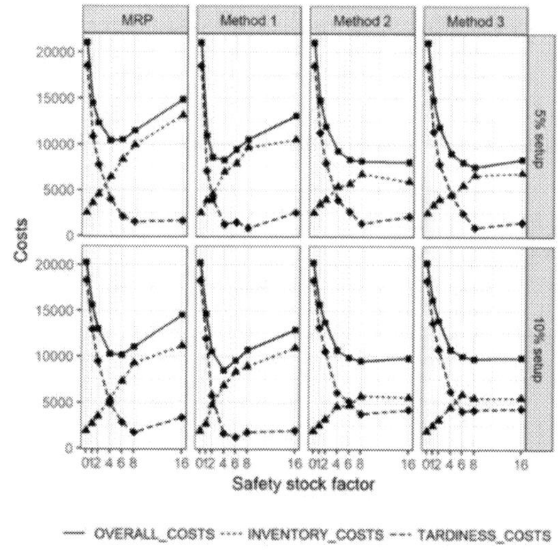

Figure 3. Influence of safety stock factor on costs.

The curves for overall costs show a clear convex shape with respect to safety stock factor, again with significant higher cost values for low safety stock values. For practical applications, this means that it is preferable to choose a higher safety stock when using safety stock relaxation, instead of selecting a safety stock that is too low. Small safety stock factors lead to high tardiness costs in comparison to inventory costs because the ability to balance capacity demands is limited. When safety stock is increased, also inventory costs increase and exceed the tardiness costs. The results show that method 1, with a lower number of safety stock relaxation occurrences, is much more sensitive on defining the right safety stock, similar to MRP. On the contrary, methods 2 and 3, i.e., more safety stock relaxation occurrences without/with memorizing this decision, can also benefit from higher safety stocks. Looking at the inventory costs shows that methods 2 and 3 also have lower inventory costs at higher safety stocks in comparison to method 1 and MRP. This implies that in methods 2 and 3 the average safety stock is lower which is intuitively clear since more safety stock relaxation occurrences are expected with these methods.

C. The Influence of FOP Periods on Safety Stock Factor

To explore the relationship between the parameters FOP periods and safety stock factor, for each value of FOP periods, the optimal safety stock factor is displayed in Figure 4. This means, that for a fixed number of FOP periods, all other parameters are varied in the predefined grid (see Table I) and the safety stock factor which leads to the minimal overall costs is selected. Again, we show all combinations of setup scenarios and methods. The optimal parameter settings presented in Table II and III are marked by a star.

In general, a lower number of FOP periods, i.e., higher overall shop load due to setup times, leads to a higher optimal safety stock factor (apart from one outlier for method 2 at 5% setup). This shows that specifically for high shop congestion, the safety stock relaxation methods demand for more safety stock in order to balance capacity better. The result for method 3 in the 10% setup scenario is interesting and shows a further increase in safety stock for a high number of FOP periods. Note that in this scenario method 3 performs significantly worse than method 1 (see also Figure 2). This implies that memorizing the safety stock reduction decision might in situations with high setup efforts and high lot covering ranges lead to system instabilities, which entail high safety stocks.

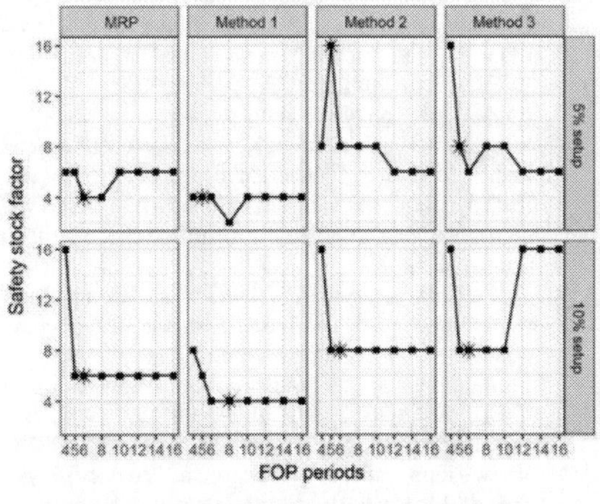

Figure 4. Influence of FOP periods on safety stock factor.

D. The Influence of Safety Stock Factor on FOP Periods

In this section we fix the safety stock factor and determine the number of FOP periods, which result in minimal overall costs. The results for all methods and scenarios are displayed in Figure 5. In six of the eight cases, the number of FOP periods show a concave shape with respect to the safety stock factor. Only for method 2 and 3 in the 10% scenarios there seems to be no influence of the safety stock on the optimal value of FOP periods. This is an interesting result since these are exactly the two scenarios where safety stock relaxation only leads to a rather small cost reduction potential (see Table III).

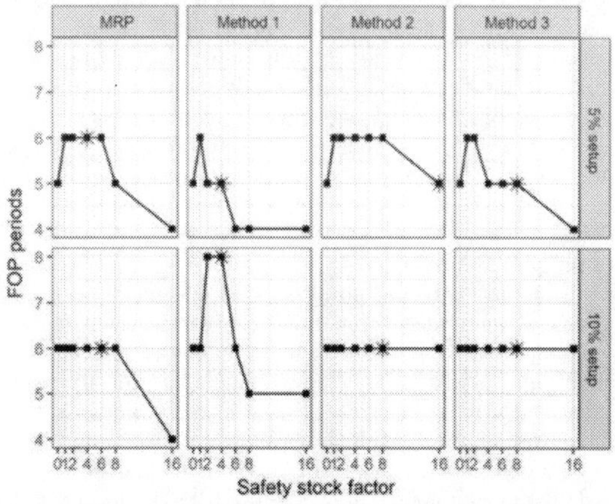

Figure 5. Influence of safety stock factor on FOP periods.

Low safety stock values lead to the situation that flexibility related to the customer demand can only be gained by lower production lot sizes. These situations still lead to high costs because no capacity load balancing is possible (see Figure 3). For medium safety stock levels, a slight increase in lot size leads to a lower overall shop load (and capacity balancing by safety stock relaxation is already possible). This lower overall utilization combined with the capacity balancing leads for most cases also to the lowest overall costs. For very high safety stock factors, high inventory costs and low tardiness costs result, i.e., customer orders can always be fulfilled from the safety stock. Therefore, lower lot sizes (lower lot covering ranges) provide a possibility to slightly decrease the inventory costs.

V. CONCLUSIONS

In this article, three methods for temporary relaxing safety stock as an extension to traditional MRP are investigated. In addition to the safety stock relaxation introduced in [16] two variations are presented and implemented in a simulation model. Since MRP neglects capacity constraints, heuristics for balancing capacity demand can improve the performance of the production system. The results of the simulation study show that all methods for safety stock relaxation lead to significant improvement in overall costs in comparison to MRP. The relative improvement ranges from 4% to 25%.

In a sensitivity analysis, the influence of the planning parameters safety stock factor and FOP periods on the performance of the production system is investigated. The overall costs in dependence of the planning parameters behave similar for method 2 and 3, because they have more common features in their functionality in contrast to method

1. One finding with practical relevance is that a higher safety stock is advantageous when relaxing safety stock, because there is only a small increase in overall costs while increasing safety stock. Opposite to this, a safety stock, which is too low, leads to considerably higher overall costs.

When exploring the interrelationship of the two planning parameters, the results show that especially for high shop loads, due to low number of FOP periods and high percentage of setup, more safety stock is needed for balancing capacity requests. In most of the cases, plotting the optimal number of FOP periods with respect to safety stock shows a concave behavior, whereby medium levels of safety stocks lead to the best solutions for overall costs. Comparing the results of method 1 to the results of methods 2 and 3 shows that method 1 is more sensitive to the safety stock factor whereas methods 2 and 3 perform significantly worse if setup times are high.

Limitations of this study are the selected ranges for the planning parameters for the grid search, which cannot guarantee an optimal solution. Furthermore, the simulation study is applied to a simple manufacturing structure. In further research, the safety stock relaxation methods have to be tested in more complex production structures or real production systems to get better estimates for the improvement potential in real world manufacturing systems.

Acknowledgment

This paper was partially funded by FFG Grant 858642 and the FH OÖ grant MCRP.

References

[1] J. Orlicky, Material requirements planning: "The new way of life in production and inventory management", McGraw-Hill, New York, 1975.

[2] T. Rossi and M. Pero, "A simulation-based finite capacity MRP procedure not depending on lead time estimation", International Journal of Operational Research, vol. 11, no. 3, 2011, pp. 237-261.

[3] L. Sun, S. S. Heragu, L. Chen, and M.L. Spearman, "Comparing dynamic risk-based scheduling methods with MRP via simulation", International Journal of Production Research, vol. 50, no. 4, 2012, pp. 921–937.

[4] M. Taal and J. C. Wortmann, "Integrating MRP and finite capacity planning", Production Planning & Control, vol. 8, no. 3, 1997, pp. 245–254.

[5] P. C. Pandey, P. Yenradee, and S. Archariyapruek, "A finite capacity material requirements planning system", Production Planning & Control, vol. 11, no. 2, 2000, pp. 113–121.

[6] N. A. Bakke and R. Hellberg, "The challenges of capacity planning", International Journal of Production Economics vol. 30-31, 1993, pp. 243–264.

[7] T. Rossi, R. Pozzi, M. Pero, and R. Cigolini, "Improving production planning through finite-capacity MRP", International Journal of Production Research vol. 55, no. 2, 2016, pp. 377–391.

[8] T. Wuttipornpun and P. Yenradee, "Development of finite capacity material requirement planning system for assembly operations", Production Planning & Control, vol. 15, no. 5, 2004, pp. 534–549.

[9] A. M. Ornek and O. Cengiz, "Capacitated lot sizing with alternative routings and overtime decisions", International Journal of Production Research, vol. 44, no. 24, 2006, pp. 5363–5389.

[10] A. R. Clark, "Optimization approximations for capacity constrained material requirements planning", International Journal of Production Economics, vol. 84, no. 2, 2003, pp. 115–131.

[11] J. Maes and L. N. van Wassenhove, "Capacitated dynamic lotsizing heuristics for serial systems", International Journal of Production Research, vol. 29, no. 6, 1991, pp. 1235-1249.

[12] L. Özdamar and T. Yazgac, "Capacity driven due date settings in make-to-order production systems", International Journal of Production Economics, vol. 49, no. 1, 1997, pp. 29–44.

[13] P. J. Billington, J. O. McClain, and L. J. Thomas, "Heuristics for Multilevel Lot-Sizing with a Bottleneck", Management Science, vol. 32, no. 8, 1986, pp. 989–1006.

[14] D. L. Woodruff and S. Voß, "A Model for Multi-Stage Production Planning with Load Dependent Lead Times", 37th Annual Hawaii International Conference on System Sciences, 2004, pp. 88–96.

[15] J. J. Kanet and M. Stößlein, "Integrating production planning and control: Towards a simple model for Capacitated ERP", Production Planning & Control 21 (3) (2010), pp. 286–300.

[16] H. Jodlbauer and S. Reitner, "Material and capacity requirements planning with dynamic lead times", International Journal of Production Research, vol. 50, no. 16, 2012, pp. 4477–4492.

[17] S. Strasser, A. Peirleitner, K. Altendorfer, C. Jenewein, and H. Jodlbauer, "The effect of safety stock relaxation and dynamic planned lead time within the MCRP algorithm in a simple manufacturing structure", unpublished.

[18] T. Felberbauer and K. Altendorfer, "Comparing the performance of two different customer order behaviors within the hierarchical production planning", in: Proceedings of the Winter Simulation Conference 2014, Institute of Electrical and Electronics Engineers, Inc., Piscataway, New Jersey, 2014, pp. 2227–2238.

[19] W. J. Hopp and M. L. Spearman, "Factory Physics", 3rd ed., Mc Graw Hill / Irwin, Boston, 2008.

[20] K. Altendorfer, "Influence of lot size and planned lead time on service level and inventory for a single-stage production system with advance demand information and random required lead times", International Journal of Production Economics, vol. 170, 2015, pp. 478–488.

Shader-Based Realtime Simulation of High-Definition Automotive Headlamps

Nico Rüddenklau, Patrick Biemelt, Sven Henning, Sandra Gausemeier and Ansgar Trächtler
Chair of Control Engineering and Mechatronics, Heinz Nixdorf Institute, University of Paderborn
33102 Paderborn, Germany
Email: {nico.rueddenklau, patrick.biemelt, sven.henning, sandra.gausemeier, ansgar.traechtler}@hni.upb.de

Abstract—**Introducing high-definition headlamp systems in the automotive industry opens up a wide range of possibilities for improving existing and developing new types of dynamic lighting functions. Due to the complexity and subjectivity of light distributions of modern headlamp systems, simulation-based development is indispensable. This paper presents a first realtime simulation of high-definition systems in virtual environments. The simulation results are evaluated using validated software for simulating static light distributions at night. The performance of the implementation on the test hardware is also discussed. First results show a great potential for future development, which will be shown at the end of the contribution.**

Keywords–high-definition headlamp; realtime headlamp simulation; night driving simulation; dynamic light distribution.

I. Introduction

Compared to other vehicle components, the development of headlamp systems is characterized by the multidimensional solution space in terms of possible light distributions and the highly subjective factor in their evaluation. A further complication is that dynamic headlamps, away from the simulation, can only be proven by time-consuming and cost-intensive night driving tests under non-reproducible test conditions. Furthermore, the construction of a prototype is expensive, therefore, it should ideally be used in late development stages only. These difficulties motivate the simulation-based development of headlamps.

Realtime simulation of headlamps was first dealt with by Kemeny et al. [1]. This initial realization implements per-vertex-lighting. The quality of the simulated light distributions therefore depends strongly on the tesselation of the scene objects. Berssenbrügge et al. present an approach based on per-fragment-lighting that decouples tesselation from the resolution of light distribution [2]. A comparable concept is presented in [3]. It utilizes a proprietary development for the simulation of night driving with additional functionalities. Based on such simulations, various publications exist for testing dynamic lighting functions. In [4], Kemeny et al. present the simulation of the cornering light function within the established driving simulation software SCANeR. Like Berssenbrügge et al. in [5], they implement predictive cornering light, which calculates the ideal light distribution on the basis of navigation data and vehicle speed. Next to the cornering light function, Berssenbrügge et al. are also testing an advanced leveling light system in their simulation environment [6]. With active safety light Knoll et al. presents the simulative testing of a new light function for highlighting possible escape ways in risky driving situations [7].

All of the implementations mentioned above have in common that the light distributions of the light sources used are static. In concrete terms, this means that they are independent of time. Dynamic functions are mapped exclusively by means of the orientation angles of the light sources. High-definition (HD) headlamps, however, realize lighting functions in a totally different way and must therefore be modelled and simulated differently. Their outstanding features and their modelling are described in Section II. Section III the shader-based implementation of the light simulation is discussed. This is divided into the determination of the total light distribution (Section III-A) and the illumination of the scene based on that (Section III-B). In Section IV, the simulation results are evaluated using a validated reference simulation tool and their performance on the utilized test hardware is examined. The last section provides a conclusion as well as recommendations for future work.

II. HD-Headlamp Systems

HD systems are characterized by a great number of independent controllable light sources. Their illumination areas concentrate on sharply defined solid angle intervals with small overlapping areas. The total light distribution of such a headlamp results from the superposition of all the individual light distributions. This architecture enables the generation of highly dynamic overall light distributions by independently controlling the electrical current of each individual light source in the headlamp. The variety of the representable light distributions is limited only by the resolution of the headlamp, which can range from approx. 100 to several 10,000 pixels, and the permissible values of the electrical current depending on the light technology used [8].

For testing the simulation presented here, the HD84-Matrix-LED-Headlamp developed by Hella KG from Lippstadt is used. The actual HD component of this headlamp is realized by a matrix of 84 LEDs, which can be supplied individually with continuously adjustable electrical current. To compensate for the relatively low resolution of 84 pixels, the illumination range of the HD module is limited to the solid angle range with the greatest variability requirements. Accordingly, additional light sources are provided to illuminate the vehicle front area, the sides and to support the high beam. In total, the HD84-Matrix-LED-Headlamp therefore has 95 light sources.

In order to simulate the light distribution in any situation, the characteristics of the emitted light must be known for each individual light source. For this purpose, so-called luminous intensity distributions are determined in lighting technology, which describe the luminous intensity of the light source depending on the direction of radiation [9]. These can be obtained for an existing headlamp by a goniophotometer-measurement [10] or for a computer model by ray tracing methods [11].

Figure 1 shows the low beam distribution of the left HD84-Matrix-LED-Headlamp. The horizontal angle θ around the vertical axis is plotted on the x-axis (0° corresponds to

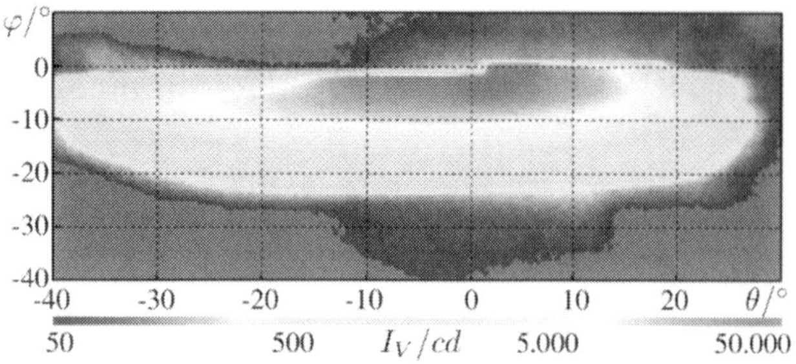

Figure 1. Low-beam distribution of luminous intensity I_V of left HD84-Matrix-LED-Headlamp measured in Candela $[cd]$.

direction of travel). Along the y-axis the vertical angle φ is plotted around the transverse axis. This is varied in the context of headlights in a much smaller range. Within the diagram, the luminous intensity I_V measured in Candela $[cd]$ is color-coded for a given pairing of horizontal and vertical angles.

In order to be able to precisely reference the relevant elements of the light distributions of HD systems in the following sections, these are described more formally. A discretized light distribution can be interpreted as a matrix whose dimensions depend on the considered angular range $[\varphi_0, \varphi_1]$ or $[\theta_0, \theta_1]$ and the corresponding resolution $\Delta\varphi$ or $\Delta\theta$ in horizontal or vertical direction, whereby $M = \frac{\varphi_1 - \varphi_0}{\Delta\varphi}, N = \frac{\theta_1 - \theta_0}{\Delta\theta} = N$ with $M, N \in \mathbb{N}$ must apply. The discrete value φ_m with $0 \leq m \leq M$ or θ_n with $0 \leq n \leq N$ then refers to the horizontal angle $\varphi_0 + m \cdot \Delta\varphi$ or the vertical angle $\theta_0 + n \cdot \Delta\theta$. The light distribution L_k of the light source k with $k \in \{1, K\}$ of an HD headlamp with a total of K individual light sources then has the form $L_k \in \mathbb{R}_{\geq 0}^{M \times N}$.

The entry $l_k(m, n)$ of row m and column n of the L_k matrix now contains the luminous intensity of the light source k in the discretized direction of the vertical angle φ_m and the horizontal angle θ_n in Candela.

After defining the light distributions of individual light sources, the aggregation of these to the total light distribution L can be formulated. For this purpose, a system is defined whose input variables represent the relative electrical current values $i_k \in [0, 1]$ of the individual light sources normalized to their maximum value. In contrast to the matrices $L_1, \ldots, L_K$, these values are time-dependent signals. The output of the system is the resulting light distribution of the headlamp and thus a weighted composition of all individual light distributions. Formally, the output variable corresponds to a L matrix whose dimensions are identical to the dimensions of the individual distributions $L_1, \ldots, L_K$. The current overall light distribution can be formulated as

$$L(t) = \sum_{k=1}^{K} i_k(t) \cdot L_k \text{ with } L(t) \in \mathbb{R}_{\geq 0}^{M \times N}. \quad (1)$$

The time-dependent matrix L now contains all information describing the light emitted by the headlamp at time t, which constitutes the basic information for simulation purposes.

III. Implementation of HD-Headlight-Simulation

The rendering of the dynamic light distributions of HD systems was realized in the development environment Unity (Version 2017.3.1f1 [12]). To ensure realtime capability in terms of a sufficient number of frames per second (fps), the high parallelism of the calculation must be exploited. For this reason, not only the lighting of the scene, but also the determination of the time-dependent total light distribution L is outsourced to the GPU, which can solve such tasks many times faster than the CPU. Consequently, both tasks are implemented as shaders in the language Cg (C for graphics) [13] and can thus be integrated into the programmable rendering pipeline [14]. First of all, it should be mentioned that because of its advantages with many light sources deferred shading is used [15]. In the following section, the generation of the total light distribution from the individual light distributions by the CookieCombiner-Shader is discussed. Afterwards the Headlight-Shader used for lighting the scene is introduced.

A. *CookieCombiner-Shader*

Textures, whose pixels correspond to the matrix entries, are used to represent the light distributions on digital level. Each pixel carries RGBA color information, with the first three channels determining its color in the RGB color space and the fourth channel (α-channel) determining the transparency of the pixel. In principle, the direction-dependent variation of the light colour would be possible via the RGB channels. In the presented solution, however, these channels are not considered, which is the reason why only monochrome light can be displayed. The directional luminous intensity is coded in the α-channel. Up to now, the texture considers an angle range of 180° in both vertical and horizontal direction and resolves in 0.2° steps. It therefore has a size of 900x900 pixels. In computer graphics, both the horizontal (u) and vertical (v) coordinates for accessing a texture and the permissible values of individual pixel information are normalized to the interval $[0, 1]$. To map the coded luminous intensity to this value range, all entries of the matrices $L_1, \ldots, L_K$ are divided by their maximum l_{max}.

Texturing of light sources to vary the luminous intensity in different beam directions is already established. Such light textures are called cookies, explaining the name of the CookieCombiner-Shader. Its task is to combine the cookies of individual light sources for total light distribution according to (1). Its render target is a cookie whose α-values are all initialized with 0. The shader is now repeatedly called on this render target and receives a single light distribution L_k and its weighting factor as parameters. In the fragment program of the shader, the α-values of the respective cookie $\alpha_{uv}(k)$ with $u, v \in [0, 1]$ are multiplied by the weighting factor and then transferred to the render target by additive blending [14]. To ensure that the α-values of the render target do not exceed the permissible value range $[0, 1]$, the weighting factor used is formed as the product of the relative electrical current i_k and the reciprocal of the total number K of all light sources. If the previous considerations are combined, the α-value α_{uv} of the render target at the normalized texture coordinates (u, v) after passing through the shader for all single light distributions is calculated as follows

$$\alpha_{uv} = \sum_{k=1}^{K} \frac{i_k}{K} \cdot \alpha_{uv}(k) = \frac{1}{K} \cdot \sum_{k=1}^{K} i_k \cdot \alpha_{uv}(k). \quad (2)$$

With (2) and $\alpha_{uv}(k), i_k \in [0, 1]$ it follows that $\alpha_{u,v}$ is also within the permissible value range. After blending, the render target contains the normalized luminous intensity of the entire headlamp. The texture coordinates correspond to the spatial directions into which the light radiates according to the explanations at the beginning of Section II. In order to reconstruct the actual luminous intensity, the normalizations required by the limited range of values must be reversed. Formally, the relationship between the original matrix entry $l(m, n)$ in L and the corresponding texture value $\alpha_{\frac{m}{M}\frac{n}{N}}$ is defined as follows

$$l(m, n) = K \cdot l_{max} \cdot \alpha_{\frac{m}{M}\frac{n}{N}}, \tag{3}$$

which ensures undistorted computational mapping of luminous intensity. The render target of the CookieCombiner-Shader represents the total light distribution of the headlamp in the form of a cookie and serves as input for the Headlight-Shader presented below.

B. Headlight-Shader

The implementation of the Headlight-Shader is much more extensive. Berssenbrügge et al. solved a similar problem in [2] by using a built-in spotlight and mapping the light distribution to its cookie scheme. The present contribution is based on Unity's built-in shader for deferred shading, but differs in the light volume, used to describe the illumination range of the headlamp, and the interpretation of the light cookie. Moreover, no shadows are rendered, as their calculation is very computation-intensive. Also, the driver and headlamps are in approximately the same position, so that shadows are hardly noticed by the driver.

Following the deferred shading procedure, the scene in the initial base path is rendered into the g-buffer (geometry buffer) independent of any lights. A very simple example of a scene is shown in Figure 2. That way, the complex 3D scene is reduced to the 2-dimensional screen output. The information relevant for lighting, such as the surface normals, depth values or color information, is stored in the g-buffer. The Headlight-Shader in the subsequent lighting pass can refer to this information.

In the lighting pass, the illumination range of the light is described by a light volume in the form of a half-sphere, which is illustrated by yellow lines in Figure 2. The light source is located in the center of the half-sphere and is oriented vertically to the plane half-spherical surface in the direction of the curvature. The light volume, approximated by a mesh of 65 vertices, is rendered, which is why the light space l is the current object space.

According to the schema of the graphics pipeline, the vertices of the mesh are first processed by the vertex program. Since the Headlight-Shader implements per-fragment-lighting, the vertex program can be realized by a few lines of code. Essentially, three parameters are generated. First, a vertex ${}_lp'$ of the light volume mesh, passed in homogeneous coordinates, is transformed from the light space l into the clip space c of the camera (line 1). The transformation from l to the world space w is done by the matrix M, from w to the view space v by the matrix V and from v to the clip space c by the matrix P (see Figure 2). c has the same origin as v, but distorts the coordinates in perspective for mapping to the screen. The vertex coordinates in the clip space ${}_cp'$ form the basis of the rasterization and must be included in the return of the vertex shader. Furthermore, the clip space position in the lines 2 and 3 is transformed so that the x and y coordinates are normalized to $[0, 1]$ for vertices in the view frustum (visible part of the scene in the form of a pyramid frustum, see thick dashed lines in Figure 2) in accordance with the perspective division in the

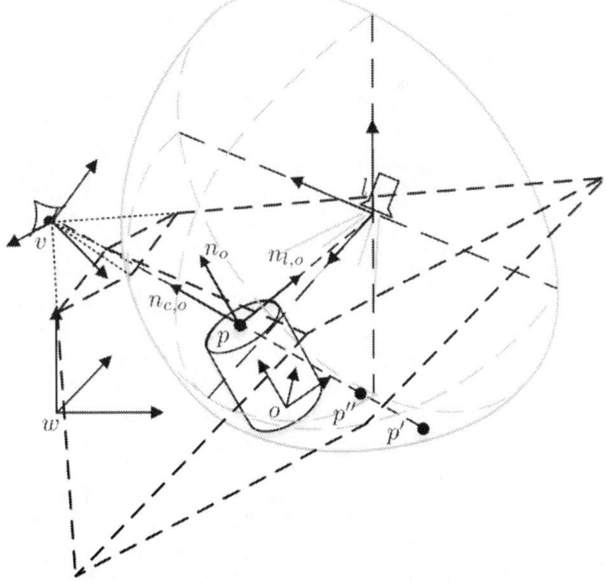

Figure 2. Simple scene to be rendered with coordinate systems for world space (w), view space (v), light space (l) and an exemplarily object with local space o.

fragment program. This information is then used to correctly address the g-buffer and forms the second output of the vertex shader. Finally, the vector from the camera to the vertex in view space ${}_vp'$ is calculated by multiplying the vertex ${}_lp'$ in l by M and V (line 4). This value is needed next to ${}_cp'_{uv}$ to reconstruct the position of the fragment in w within the fragment shader and forms the third return of the vertex shader. This way all vertices of the half sphere are processed by the shader.

Require: ${}_lp' \in \mathbb{R}^4$ vertex of light volume as homogeneus coordinates in l

1: ${}_cp' \leftarrow P \cdot V \cdot M \cdot {}_lp'$ // vertex in c
2: ${}_cp'_{uv}.x \leftarrow \frac{1}{2} \cdot {}_cp'.x + \frac{1}{2} \cdot {}_cp'.w$ // transform to screen space
3: ${}_cp'_{uv}.y \leftarrow \frac{1}{2} \cdot {}_cp'.y + \frac{1}{2} \cdot {}_cp'.w$ // transform to screen space
4: ${}_vp' \leftarrow V \cdot M \cdot {}_lp'$ // vertex in v
5: **return** ${}_cp', {}_cp'_{uv}, {}_vp'$

Afterwards the rasterization is effected based on the clip space coordinates ${}_cp'$. The remaining vertex program returns are interpolated to the fragments according to their distances to the vertices. The fragment shader is called for all fragments covered by the light volume with the respective interpolation results ${}_cp'_{uv}, {}_vp'$.

Require: ${}_cp'_{uv} \in \mathbb{R}^4$ transformed coords in c and ${}_vp' \in \mathbb{R}^3$ coords in v of vertex p' of light volume

1: ${}_vp'' \leftarrow \frac{f}{{}_vp'.z} \cdot {}_vp'$ // scale to far clipping distance (f)
2: $b_{uv} \leftarrow \frac{1}{{}_cp'_{uv}.w} \cdot {}_cp'_{uv}.xy$ // buffer coords of p' (same for p)
3: $z_{uv} \leftarrow G_{depth}(b_{uv})$ // norm. depth at screen position b_{uv}
4: ${}_vp \leftarrow z_{uv} \cdot {}_vp''$ // position of p in v
5: ${}_wp \leftarrow V^{-1} \cdot {}_vp$ // position of p in w
6: ${}_wv_{c,o} \leftarrow {}_wp_c - {}_wp_o$ // vector p→camera in w
7: ${}_wn_{c,o} \leftarrow \frac{{}_wv_{c,o}}{|{}_wv_{c,o}|}$ // direction p→camera in w

8: ${}_wl \leftarrow M[1:4, 4]$ // position of light in w
9: ${}_wv_{l,o} \leftarrow {}_wl - {}_wp$ // vector p→light in w
10: ${}_wn_{l,o} \leftarrow \frac{{}_wv_{l,o}}{|{}_wv_{l,o}|}$ // direction p→light in w

11: ${}_{l}p \leftarrow L \cdot {}_{w}p$ // vector light→p in l
12: $a_{deg}.x \leftarrow \text{atan2}({}_{l}p.x, {}_{l}p.z)$ // horiz. and vert. angle be-
13: $a_{deg}.y \leftarrow \text{atan2}({}_{l}p.y, {}_{l}p.z)$ // tween light axis and ${}_{l}p$
14: $a_{uv} \leftarrow \frac{a_{deg}+90^{\circ}}{180^{\circ}}$ // Light-Cookie coordinates
15: $l_{uv} \leftarrow T_{cookie}(a_{uv})$ // light power in specific direction

16: $att \leftarrow \frac{1}{l.range^2} \cdot {}_{w}v_{l,o} \cdot {}_{w}v_{l,o}$ // light attenuation
17: $att \leftarrow att \cdot l_{uv}$ // consider light power
18: $l.color \leftarrow att \cdot l.color$ // attenuated light color

19: **return** lightingModel($c_o, {}_{w}n_o, {}_{w}n_{c,o}, {}_{w}n_{l,o}, l.color$)

The shader code can be divided into five logical blocks. The first block (line 1 to 7) reconstructs the three dimensional surface point p of the scene object o visible on the current fragment. This reconstruction is enabled by the additional information provided by the vertex shader. The vector p' is mapped to the same screen position as p (see dashed line through p, p' and p'' in Figure 2). Therefore ${}_{v}p'$ describes the cameras view direction to p in v. The g-buffer created in the base path of deferred shading can be used to determine the exact position of p on the corresponding line. It encodes the z coordinate in v for each fragment in addition to other data. To read the correct value from the depth buffer, the buffer coordinates must be determined first. Therefore the vector ${}_{c}p'_{uv}$ is defined in the vertex shader, whose x- and y-coordinates lie in the interval $[0, {}_{c}p'_{v}.w = {}_{c}p'_{uv}.w]$ for points within view frustum. After the perspective division by the homogeneous component in line 2 the coordinates b_{uv} are in the value range $[0, 1]$ (line 3) used for texture/buffer access. The depth buffer encodes depth z_{uv} normalized on distance f to the far clipping plane in the interval $[0, 1]$. The coords of p in v result from scaling of ${}_{v}p'$ to the far clipping plane receiving ${}_{v}p''$ (line 1) and the subsequent multiplication with the normalized depth z_{uv} (line 4). Multiplication by the inverse of V transfers the object point p from v to w. For the evaluation of the lighting model, the normalized direction vector from the object point to the camera (eye vector) in world space ${}_{w}n_{o,c}$ (see Figure 2) is needed (line 6 and 7).

In addition to the eye vector, the incidence of light on the object plays a central role in the lighting model, too. The light vector is defined in lines 8 to 10. First the position of the light source in world space ${}_{w}l$ is extracted from the matrix M (line 8). Since the Headlight-Shader only renders the mesh of the light volume into the light buffer, the transformation matrix M from current object space l to w is constant across all calls of the vertex program and contains the translation, rotation and scaling of the light volume mesh into w. Since the light source is in the coordinate origin of l, the translation in M corresponds to the position of the light in w and can be read from the fourth column of M. Now the normalized direction vector from the object point to the light source in world space ${}_{w}n_{l,o}$ (see Figure 2) can be determined by the lines 9 and 10 similar to the previous section.

In the lines 11 to 15, the directional luminous intensity generated as cookie (T_{cookie}) in the CookieCombiner-Shader is taken into account. In order to determine the luminous intensity to be applied to the current fragment from the light distribution, the horizontal and vertical angles of the incident light beam with respect to the light centre axis must be calculated. For this purpose, the object point belonging to the fragment is transferred to the light space l through multiplying by L. The position of this point in l, in whose coordinate origin the light source is located and oriented along the z axis, simultaneously corresponds to the light beam ${}_{l}p$ from the source to the object. Its angle to the light center axis or z axis in l can then be determined with the $atan2$ function (line 12 and 13). The cookie must be addressed with normalized texture coordinates. Therefore, the angles moving in the range $[-90^{\circ}, +90^{\circ}]$ due to the used light volume are transformed by line 14 to texture coordinates a_{uv}. Thereby, the applicable value can finally be read out by the light distribution (line 15).

After the positions of the relevant elements and the luminous intensity of the light are already known, the distance to the light source must be taken into account in the lines 16 to 18. The intensity of light decreases square with the distance to the shined object [16]. This square distance can be formulated most efficiently as a scalar product of the vector from object to light ${}_{w}v_{l,o}$ with itself. The distance between object and light is referred to a freely selectable positive light parameter $l.range$, which allows the user to adjust the range respectively the intensity of the light (line 16). It applies $att = 1$ if the distance between light source and object corresponds to the parameter $l.range$, and $att \rightarrow \infty$ for increasing distances. To take into account the directional luminous intensity l_{uv}, which is normalized to the interval $[0, 1]$, att is multiplied by this value. The calculated light attenuation can finally be mapped by the light color in line 18 through multiplying the color of the light defined by the user by att. Assuming a white light, this multiplication corresponds to a shift on the grayscale.

Finally, the lighting model can be evaluated. At this point, no separate solution has been implemented yet, but a Unity-internal local lighting model has been used. This receives the previously determined normals ${}_{w}n_{o,c}$, ${}_{w}n_{l,o}$, the surface normal ${}_{w}n_o$ (see Figure 2) and material data c_o of the object from the g buffer and the light color $l.color$, which already considers attenuation. Based on these data, the lighting model delivers the resulting color for the currently considered fragment and thus generates the finished image of the scene on the output medium.

IV. RESULTS

After the implementation is presented, the results are evaluated in terms of subjective appearance and computation time.

A. Appearance

A strictly objective evaluation based on numerical measurements apart from the legal requirements is difficult in the context of headlighting. Instead, a subjective comparison of the implemented simulation and the LightDriver software from Hella KG (64 Bit Version built on Jul, 2017) is used as the primary evaluation basis. LightDriver is a validated software tool for simulating headlamp light in night driving, which Hella KG uses for its own development work. In contrast to the implementation presented here, the LightDriver is not able to display the high dynamics of HD systems in realtime, since it has been primarily designed for the representation of static light distributions. However, they are sufficient for the plausibility check concerning the appearance of the presented implementation and serve as a reference.

Figure 3 compares the dipped beam distribution of the HD84-Matrix-LED-Headlamp as calculated by

Figure 3. Low-beam light of HD84-Matrix-LED-Headlamp projected on a street with auxiliary surfaces simulated with own implementation (top) and LightDriver (bottom).

CookieCombiner- and Headlight-Shader with the light distribution of the LightDriver as reference. While in the presented implementation only the electrical current values of the individual light sources belonging to this light distribution are specified, the LightDriver requires a simpler input in the form of a single light distribution, which is therefore calculated in advance. The scene for this comparison could not be taken directly from the LightDriver and was therefore recreated. As a consequence the geometric dimensions, textures and colours of scene objects are not exactly the same, but should suffice for a plausibility check.

At first glance you can see that the overall brightness differ between both images. This difference is due to the different textures. On closer inspection, one notices that the LightDriver shows weak light curtains in the vehicle apron, which are not reproduced in the implementation presented. There are also qualitative differences in distance-dependent light attenuation. The reasons for this are on the one hand the too coarse resolution of 8 bit (α-channel of a RGBA texture) used for the luminous intensity and on the other hand the different light models. Essentially, however, there is a strong similarity between the light distributions of both simulations. They have comparable expansions and the same qualitative profile. If one looks at the auxiliary surfaces at the left and right edge of the road, it is noticeable that both light distributions illuminate one's own side of the road much more strongly in the distance than the one next to it. This is a classic feature of low-beam light distributions that ensures that oncoming traffic is not glared.

Even if the light distribution on the road is the central evaluation criterion for the driver, the observation of light distributions on a vertical measuring wall has proven to be useful especially for comparison purposes. The contours of the light distribution, which are called the light-dark boundary in this context, become clear through the close projection of distant areas.

Although on Figure 4 both measuring walls are each 10 meters away, different distances seem to be present. This impression is deceptive because of different road textures leading to a distorted perception, especially due to the positions

Figure 4. Low-beam light of HD84-Matrix-LED-Headlamp simulated with own implementation (top) and LightDriver (bottom) on a measurement wall.

of the central strips. In addition, the parameters of the camera are not known in the LightDriver and therefore there is a different view frustum in the implementation presented here. The already mentioned disadvantages of the too low resolution of the presented implementation are expressed by a sharper light-dark boundary. Apart from these inequalities the vertical projection shows the similarity of both simulations even clearer than Figure 3. They have a dipped beam typical border to the left in the upper middle area. The high resolution of the HD system allows a sharp cut along the vertical center line and thus ensures optimum long-range illumination of one's own lane without restricting other traffic participants. In addition to the comparison shown, the high beam distribution was also tested with a high degree of consistency.

B. Computation Time

With regard to the realtime requirement, the performance of the implementation has to be taken into account. Our workstation PC, which is representative for current average computers, as test hardware is sufficient for a fundamental evaluation of the realtime capability. This is a 64bit Windows 10 system with an Intel Core i7-6820HQ CPU (2.7 GHz, 8 cores), 16GB RAM and an NVIDIA Quadro M3000M with 4GB VRAM. The runtime of the rendering can be classified as sufficient, if the calculation of the entire scene can be carried out at least with the maximum frame rate of 60 fps of a classical output device.

The independent evaluation of the performance of the Headlight-Shader is only conditionally meaningful due to the many influences, which result from the non realtime capable operating system, the test hardware and the measurement itself. For this reason, the implemented lights are compared with Unity Spotlights, which represent the light sources with the most similar properties. A large, flat surface serves as a test scenario. In the middle of it, the camera is oriented parallel to the ground. The scene can be rendered in 6.11 ms (164 fps). In front of the camera position, 50 Unity Spotlights are placed and parameterized with a range of 60 length units and a spot angle of 179° (max. value). The central axis of the light corresponds to the direction of the camera's view. The calculation time is recorded over 1000 frames. The average value for the calculation of a frame is 9.78 ms (102 fps). In the same scenario, the Unity Spotlights are now replaced by as many lights from the implementation presented here with the same range parameter. In this case, the average calculation time is 19.60 ms (51 fps). After subtraction of the rendering of the unexposed scene, 0.07 ms per Unity Spotlight and 0.27 ms per headlamp are required. Even if the Headlight-Shader turns out to be slower than a Unity Spotlight, it is suitable for realtime simulation even including external traffic. In particular, the computing time is not negatively affected by more complex scenes, but depends only on the resolution of the output device (here 1354x873 pixels) due to the use of deferred shading.

In addition to the Headlight-Shader, the performance of the CookieCombiner-Shader must be checked. The headlamp ECU (Electronic Control Unit) is clocked at 50 Hz, so that a recalculation in each frame should be assumed for the CookieCombiner-Shader. Due to the difficulties in measuring computing time mentioned in the previous section, an artificial test scenario is also created for the CookieCombiner-Shader. To obtain the most representative value possible, 1,000 total light distributions of the HD84-Matrix-LED-Headlamp are determined by iteration. Since the shader is called once per single light distribution, this corresponds to 95,000 calls of the CookieCombiner-Shader. The average calculation time of a total light distribution is 0.304 ms. Accordingly, CookieCombiner- and Headlight-Shader use a comparable amount of resources, so that a total of 0.6 ms is required for the calculation of a headlamp. Considering complex scenes and the integration of external traffic, further optimization potentials should be researched.

V. Conclusion and Future Work

This contribution presents an approach for realtime simulation of dynamic HD headlamp systems and thus lays the foundation for the simulation-based development of high-resolution dynamic light functions. Taking into account the rather average test hardware and the optimization possibilities discussed below, the shader-based implementation shows potential to simulate night driving with dynamic HD system in reduced scenes.

The rendering of the headlight is divided into two steps. In the first step, the current total light distribution is determined. This is the weighted sum of the 95 individual light distributions of all adjustable light sources of the HD84-Matrix-LED-Headlamp. In the technical implementation, the light distributions are represented by textures with a resolution of 900x900 pixels and superimposed by blending the results of the CookieCombiner-Shader applied to them. The total light distribution initiates the second rendering step as input for the Headlight-Shader. In the lighting pass of deferred shading, this shader determines the final color values of the output device pixels, taking into account the light influences.

The LightDriver software from Hella KG is used to evaluate the results. As a tool for headlamp development that has been established for years, it is an excellent reference. As the Figures 3 and 4 show, the implemented simulation is similar to the LightDriver. The differences can mainly be traced back to the unequal scenes and light models, as well as the differently resolved light intensity. The last two points are starting points for future work.

The performance analysis shows that Headlight- and CookieCombiner-Shader are of comparable complexity and lead to a calculation time of 0.6 ms per headlamp. For driving simulations with the integration of external traffic, these execution times should be further reduced. Therefore two ideas could be persued. On the one hand, the previously considered angular range in the vertical dimension could be reduced from $[-90°, +90°]$ to about $[+10°, -25°]$ without hiding relevant areas of the light distribution. This would decrease the required pixels per cookie significant, reducing computing operations and memory required. A more sophisticated coding of the light distribution including additional color channels could also be considered to reduce memory and increase the resolution of the luminous intensity. On the other hand, it would be possible to segment the calculation of the total light distribution to divide it into several frames. However, this way only the frame rate, not the update rate of the light distribution can be increased.

Acknowledgment

The authors would like to thank Hella KG for providing the light distribution data of the HD84-Matrix-LED-Headlamp and the LightDriver simulation software. This paper is part of the EFRE.NRW (European Fonds for Regional Development, North Rhine-Westphalia)-funded project 'Smart Headlamp Technology (SHT)'.

References

[1] P. Lecocq, J.-M. Kelada, and A. Kemeny, "Interactive Headlight Simulation," Driving Simulation Conference, 1999.

[2] J. Berssenbrügge, J. Gausemeier, G. M., C. Matysczok, and K. Pöhland, "Real-Time Representation of Complex Lighting Data in a Nightdrive Simulation," 7. International Immersive Projection Technologies Workshop, 9. Eurographics Workshop on Virtual Environments, 2003.

[3] J. Löwenau and M. Strobl, "Advanced Lighting Simulation (ALS) for the Evaluation of the BMW System Adaptive Light Control (ALC)," International Body Engineering Conference & Exhibition and Automative & Transportation Technology Conference, 2002.

[4] A. Kemeny et al., "Application of real-time lighting simulation for intellignet front-lighting studies," Driving Simulation Conference, 2000.

[5] J. Berssenbrügge, J. Bauch, and J. Gausemeier, "A Virtual Reality-based Night Drive Simulator for the Evaluation of a Predictive Advanced Front Lighting System," Design Engineering Technical Conferences & Computers and Information in Engineering Conference, 2006.

[6] J. Berssenbrügge, S. Kreft, and J. Gausemeier, "Virtual Prototyping of an Advanced Leveling Light System Using a Virtual Reality-Based Night Drive Simulator," Journal of Computing and Information Science in Engineering, 2010.

[7] A. Knoll et al., "Evaluation of an Active Safety Light using Virtual Test Drive within Vehicle In The Loop," IEEE International Conference on Industrial Technology, 2010.

[8] "AutomobilIndustrie: Adaptives LCD-Licht mit 30.000 Pixeln (Automotive Industry: Adaptive LCD-Light with 30,000 Pixels)," 2017, URL: https://www.automobil-industrie.vogel.de/index.cfm?pid=1&pk=629502&p=1 [retrieved: 8, 2018].

[9] K. Reif, Ed., Automobilelektronik (Automotive Electronics). Vieweg+Teubner, GWV Fachverlage GmbH, Wiesbaden, 2009, ISBN: 978-3-8348-0446-4.

[10] H.-H. P. Wu, Y.-P. Lee, and S.-H. Chang, "Fast measurement of automotive headlamps based on high dynamic range imaging," OSA Applied Optics Vol. 51, 2012.

[11] A. S. Glassner, Ed., An Introduction to Ray Tracing. ACADEMIC PRESS INC., San Diego, CA 92101, 1989, ISBN: 0-12-286160-4.

[12] "Unity Homepage," URL: https://unity3d.com/ [retrieved: 8, 2018].

[13] R. Fernando and M. J. Kilgard, Eds., The Cg Tutorial: The Definitive Guide to Programmable Real-Time Graphics. Addison Wesley Pub Co Inc., Feb. 2003, ISBN: 978-0321194961.

[14] J. F. Hughes et al., Eds., Computer Graphics - Principles and Practice, 3th Edition. Addison-Wesley, Jul. 2013, ISBN: 978-0321399526.

[15] T. Saito and T. Takahashi, "Comprehensible Rendering of 3-D Shapes," SIGGRAPH '90, Dallas, 1990.

[16] F. Pedrotti, L. Pedrotti, W. Bausch, and H. Schmidt, Eds., Optik für Ingenieure - Grundlagen, 4. Auflage (Optics for Engineers - Basics, 4th edition). Springer, Berlin, 2007, ISBN: 9783540734710.

Simulation and Long Term (Military) Manpower Planning: a Custom Generic Simulation Tool

Johan Van Kerckhoven (corresponding author)
Oussama Mazari-Abdessameud, Filip Van Utterbeeck

Dept. of Mathematics (MWMW)
Koninklijke Militaire School
Brussels, Belgium
Email: johan.vankerckhoven@mail.be

Abstract—**This article presents a discrete event simulation tool/engine, which we are currently developing in Julia – making use of the SimJulia package – to assist with long term manpower management of our organization. Although this tool is inspired by one particular case, our ultimate goal is to make this tool as generic and configurable as possible, while also being easy to use. We go into some detail about the inner workings of the tool, highlight its current capabilities, and elaborate on the technologies used to develop it and on how users, both expert and casual, can interact with the tool. At each point, we highlight the features that are still in development, and the points where the tool requires improvement.**

Keywords*–*Manpower simulation; manpower planning; discrete event simulation; in development.

I. Introduction

In this day and age, proper human resource management becomes more and more important for organizations of all kinds. First of all, managers need to balance the requirements of their organization with the needs and wants of their employees. In addition to that, they must be able to make well-informed planning decisions to ensure the smooth (future) operation of the organization.

These planning decisions cover different time horizons. Long term planning, which is the focus of this article, deals with hiring and promotion strategies to meet the organizations goals without alienating the employees, or compensating for and adjusting to changing legal constraints, for example an increase in the minimum retirement age. Short term workforce planning on the other hand covers among others, setting up employee rosters such that the workload is appropriately distributed over the employees, taking into account shift preferences of particular employees, absences due to time off or illness, and legal constraints.

These long term planning decisions are too important to be left solely to the managers gut feeling. Instead, they can choose to employ one or several mathematical models to provide valuable insights towards making appropriate decisions. Managers have a wide range of models available to them for this task, including Markov models (f.ex. [1] and [2]), optimization models using mathematical programming (f.ex. [3]), simulation models (f.ex. [4] and [5]), and system dynamics models (f.ex. [6]). Each of these approaches can be used to model the transient states or the steady states of the system, and every approach has its particular advantages, and drawbacks, for these tasks.

Due to an upcoming reorganization, the Belgian military is currently faced with such a long term planning problem, and the choice was made to use a simulation-driven stochastic optimization routine. This would allow the user to capture as many of the peculiarities of the organization as desired. In addition to the flexibility of the model, several other factors were taken into account to influence the choice of which particular tool to use. These factors included computation speed, financial cost, and user friendliness, by which we mean that it can be used relatively easily by non-experts. Of the investigated solutions that were available at the time, none satisfied these criteria to a sufficient degree. Hence, the decision was made to develop our own solution in the programming Julia [7], based on the SimJulia package [8], with the express goal of making the tool as flexible, generic, and user-friendly as possible.

This article presents the current state of the tool, which is still in very active development. In particular, we are developing a library of functions, which will allow the user to set up an entire workforce organization, or a part thereof, with all its HR policies (recruitment, promotion/transfer, retirement) in place. The user can then perform a simulation run to see how the composition of the workforce will evolve over time, taking the policies into account, and to generate easily digestible reports on the evolution (of any desired part) of the workforce. These simulation results and reports can then be used as a basis for a stochastic optimization routine to find the optimal set of HR policies for a particular organizational goal. However, the optimization part falls outside the scope of this article. Parallel to the simulator engine, we are also developing a user-friendly way of configuring a simulation, to allow non-expert users to set up and run a simulation in a relatively straightforward manner.

The article is structured in the following manner. In Section II, we describe the setup of the simulation model, where we highlight the current, as of writing, state of the model. The next section, Section III, covers the software and technologies used to implement the simulation tool, as well as the reasoning behind it. In Section IV, we explain how the simulation tool can be used, where the focus will be on the "non-expert" user. In each of these sections we also mention what features of the tool are still planned. Section V gives a small example of the present capabilities of the simulation tool. Finally, we briefly summarize in Section VI.

II. Setup of the Simulation Model

We have opted to build the simulation model as a discrete event simulation where we model each individual personnel member with their own attributes in the system. The simulation then allows each person to move through the system and their attributes to change based on the organization's policies, legal requirements included, as provided by the user.

The rest of the section goes into more detail on each of the three flows that a person in the simulation will undergo:

1) Flow in – recruitment
2) Flow through/transitions – transfers, promotions, etc.
3) Flow out – retirement, resignation, other forms of attrition

Please note that, as the tool is still under active development, and in a rather early stage at that, the features described below are not set in stone, and that the actual approach towards implementing these can still change considerably.

A. Entering the system

Persons can enter the organization in two ways. First of all, they can be recruited into the organization throughout the simulation run time; alternatively, the simulation can start with an existing population (start from a snapshot).

1) Recruitment: Recruitment happens in periodic recruitment cycles throughout the simulation: every few time steps a number of people will be generated and entered into the organization. Hence, instant recruitment the moment a person is needed is not allowed. The main reason for this choice is that in real life applications, it is impossible to recruit a person at any given moment. This is in part due to the organization's policies, and in part due to practical considerations: if recruitment at any moment were permitted, it'd mean that every recruit would (potentially) need a personal training schedule and trainer.

At the start of each cycle, the number of people to recruit is determined. This can either be a fixed number, a number drawn from a user provided distribution, or a number determined by the needs of the system, where this number can vary between certain bounds.

When a person is generated in the system, all their attributes are initialized to appropriate values, where those attributes and the initial distribution of those values are provided by the user. This includes the person's age upon recruitment.

Currently, implementation of the recruitment process has been mostly completed. That is to say, it is possible to set up multiple recruitment schemes as described above. However, all those recruitment schemes will use the same distributions for the initial values of the generated persons: differentiation between recruitment schemes is not possible yet.

2) Snapshot: The snapshot, i.e. starting from an inital population, has not been implemented yet.

B. Transitions

Transitions are nothing more than a change of a state that a person in the simulation can have. We have defined a state as a collection of attributes that must have specific values. Note that these states need not be mutually exclusive. For example: a person in a military organization can be an officer, be part of the ground forces, etc. We also aim at allowing states to have their own specific attributes, such as name (already implemented), and the number of people preferred to be in this state (to be implemented).

Just as with recruitment, transitions are assumed to happen periodically, where each transition has its own cycle. Currently, we only allow that these transitions happen automatically after a set period of time. In the near future, we wish to implement that these transitions have a certain probability of occurring, and that each person has a set number of chances of undergoing the transition. In addition, we will also implement that each transition has a set of extra conditions, not expressed in the initial state, that need to be satisfied before the transition can take place. For example, to become a helicopter pilot, a person must be in the air force, and have a certain rank (state), but they must also have a certificate that they can actually operate a helicopter and not be older than a certain age (extra conditions).

C. Leaving the system

Similar to recruitment, there are two ways to leave the system: retirement and attrition, where attrition covers everything from voluntary resignation to forced resignation due to medical reasons.

1) Retirement: At present, retirement occurs on a periodic schedule, similar to recruitment, and is defined by age and career length. If a person reaches a certain age, they have to retire, and similar if their career reaches a certain length. Currently, there is one retirement schedule, which is valid for all people in the simulation. In a later stage, we will allow for different retirement policies for different groups of people.

2) Attrition: Attrition is defined as a probability, per period, that a person will leave the organization for any reason except mandatory retirement. If a person will leave the organization during the next attrition period, an exponential distribution is used to determine the exact time they leave. This attrition probability can change during the lifetime of a person, for example, people will leave the organization much more frequently in the early stages of their career. As with retirement, it is not yet possible to configure different attrition schemes for different groups of people, but this is, again, a planned feature.

III. Technical Choices and Motivation

We have chosen to develop the software in the programming language Julia [7], a high-level, high-performance, open source programming language for numerical computing which is developed at MIT. In particular, we rely on its SimJulia package [8] for setting up discrete event simulations. This package manages simulated time, the event queue etc. while our own package builds on top of that.

We chose to use the Julia language due to the in house experience available, and due to its ease of use and computational speed, which in many cases rivals that of C [9]. In addition to this, benchmark tests by the developer of SimJulia have consistently shown that this package is computationally the most performant tool to drive a discrete event simulation, outpacing other implementations sometimes by an order of magnitude. Considering the intended application of the manpower simulation tool and the size of the organization for which it is intended, computational performance is essential. The final reason for choosing Julia is its open source character, which allows us to determine what's going on behind the scenes, and tailor the optimization to it.

To store the data generated throughout the simulation, we rely on an SQLite [10] database, which we access through the SQLite package [11] of Julia. This is an implementation of SQL which does not rely on a database server and client-server interactions. Instead, it uses a file saved locally, which means we do not have to rely on the availability of the connection between the machine which runs the Julia code, and the server housing the database of simulation results. An additional benefit is of course speed (again), as local files are generally available nearly instantaneously, especially when using a solid state drive. A roadblock here was the large number of SQLite calls, resulting in a large number of time-intensive file operations. However, we have circumvented this issue by keeping the database in memory and only saving it to file at certain points throughout the simulation.

IV. Using the simulation tool

This section gives a brief overview of the ways the user can configure a manpower simulation in this tool, and how they can extract information once a simulation is completed.

A. Configuration

The tool is being developed in such a way that every aspect of a manpower simulation can either be configured from a more-or-less user friendly Excel file, or from Julia itself through the use of various configuration functions. The first configuration method is intended for the non-expert user who wishes to evaluate a certain scenario (set of manpower management policies), whereas the second method, configuring a simulation straight from Julia, is more intended for developers who wish to use this simulation tool as a driver for their own manpower planning tools, for example an optimization tool.

B. Output

As indicated above, the results of the simulation are stored in an SQLite database. This database holds a record of all the entities in the simulation (past and present), as well as all the state changes and changes to entity attribute that have occurred during this simulation.

To extract intelligible information from this database, we provide several functions which generate simple reports on the following:

- Size of the population, or a specified subpopulation, at a regular time grid. These counts can be broken down by the values of a specified attribute, for example a breakdown of all air force personnel by rank category (enlisted, non com, officer).
- Flux in/out of the population or a specified subpopulation, on regular time intervals. By flux in we mean that a person is not part of the (sub)population at the start of an interval, and they are part of it at the end of that interval, similarly for flux out. These fluxes can either be broken down by source/target state, or by transition.

These reports are produced in an easily accessible Julia data structure, and can be used as they are by developers for further processing. Alternatively, the user can request a variety of plots to be compiled based on these reports, where the request is made through the Excel file:

- Line plot of the totals;
- Line plot of the breakdowns of the population and/or the in/out fluxes;
- Stacked area plots of the breakdowns;
- Percentage area plots of the breakdowns.

These plots allow the user to see, at a glance, the workforce's composition, and to gauge whether a particular set of HR policies leads to a stable organization or a constantly varying situation.

TABLE I. Attributes and Initial Distribution.

Grade cat	prob	BDL	prob
Vol	60%	Limited	100%
NonCom	30%	Appointed	0%
Off	10%		

TABLE II. Transitions.

Start – Target	Time (y)
Vol + Limited – Vol + Appointed	6y
NonCom + Limited – NonCom + Appointed	8y
Off + Limited – Off + Appointed	10y
Vol + Appointed – NonCom + Appointed	12y
NonCom + Appointed – Off + Appointed	12y

Finally, it is also possible to request a graphical representation of the system or part thereof, such that the user can get an idea of how people can move through this system. With this representation it is of course important to keep in mind that entities in the simulation can be in several states at the same time.

Towards the future, we will also allow the user to export this graphical representation to graphML such that it can be consulted in greater detail through the use of software, such as yEd [12], or to other common graph representation formats.

V. Example

In this section, we provide a small, highly unrealistic(!), example of the current capabilities of the tool. The example itself is described in Section V-A, and the results are summarized in Section V-B.

A. Description

The simulation settings that we use in the example assume an organization with a target size of 25,000 people, simulated over 50 years, and two recruitment schemes. The first scheme recruits a random number of people, between 400 and 500, every 12 months from the start of the simulation, and the second scheme recruits anywhere between 300 and 500 people depending on how many are needed still, every 12 months starting 6 months into the simulation. Ages are chosen randomly between 18 and 25 years.

We consider two attributes to be of importance, and these are listed in Table I along with the probability of each value on person recruitment. 'Grade cat' is the grade category, and BDL means limited duration, implying a person is not guaranteed to be allowed to stay in the organization after completing a sort of "trial" period. The possible states are all the possible combinations of these two attributes, and the only transitions allowed are the ones listed in Table II.

Persons in the simulation retire at 67 years of age or after a 45 year long career, and they have a 4% chance per year to resign during the first 4 years of their career, 2% until 20 years of tenure, and 1% thereafter.

B. Results

The runtime of the simulation is around 65 seconds with observed variation of $\pm$ 3 seconds between simulation runs on a single core of a 2.70 GHz (max. turbo 3.70 GHz) processor. A more detailed breakdown of the computation time, listing what percentage of the time is used for each task, is not available at present.

The breakdown of the population (stacked + percentage) is shown in Figure 1. From the top plot, which shows the

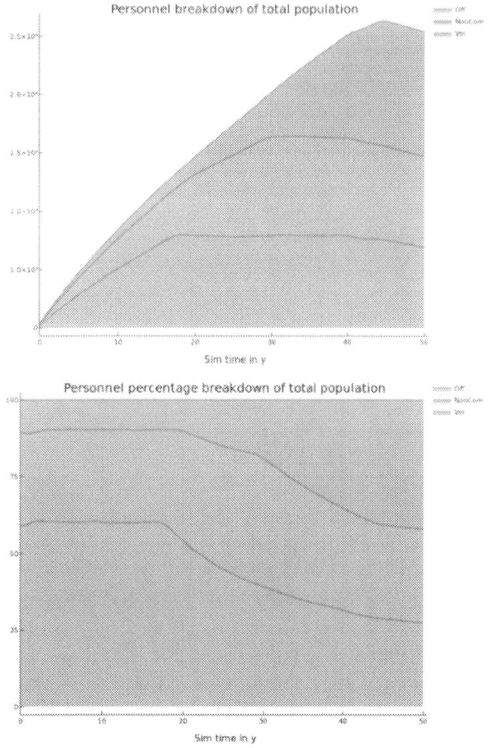

Figure 1. Breakdown of population by rank category.

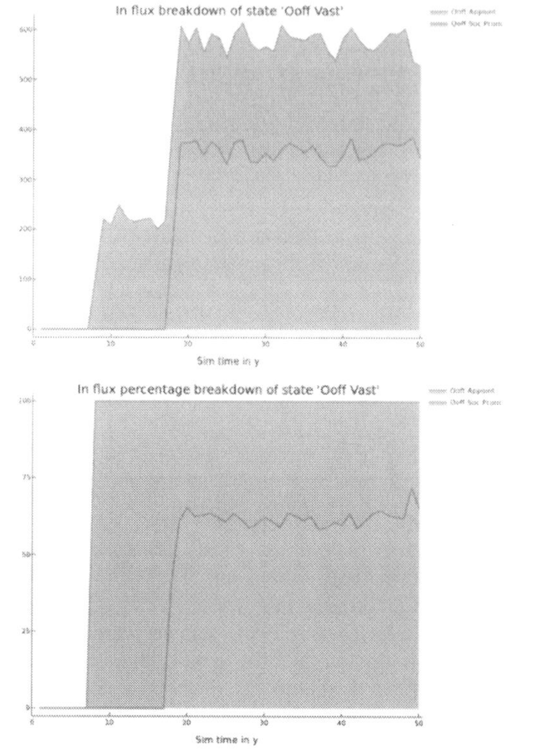

Figure 2. Breakdown of influx into the state NonCom + Appointed.

breakdown per grade category, we observe that the total population steadily rises to a level somewhat above 25,000 before slowly decreasing towards it. It we would have run the simulation for longer, we would see that the population will stabilize around this number with some fluctuations. The percentage breakdown plot (bottom) shows that the ratios of the different grade categories are as expected at the start, until the promotions start to kick in, leading to a vastly skewed population composition after 50 years, which we would expect from the way this simulation was set up.

Figure 2 shows information of the influx into the state of 'Ooff Vast' (NonCom + appointed). The breakdown of this influx shows that the first influx into this category comes from the people who are NonCom and get their appointment (Ooff Appoint), but some time later a second influx is added to this, from the people who are Vol + Appointed (Ooff Soc Prom). The percentage breakdown plot shows that the latter type of influx becomes the dominant one. This is but a small sample of all the information that can be extracted from even this simple example, and serves to give some idea of the potential uses for this simulation tool.

VI. Conclusion

We are currently developing a generic simulation tool to assist with making manpower planning decisions, which can be used either for evaluating specific scenarios as well as serve as a driver for optimization routines to determine an optimal policy. In its present state, the tool is nearly functionally complete, where most features have been implemented albeit in a restricted form. As such, we wish and are encouraged to develop this tool further such that the additional extensions, mostly related to the flixibility and genericity of the tool, mentioned in the article are present in the final product, without excessively sacrificing the performance of the tool.

Acknowledgment

The authors would like to thank Guy Van Acker for his valuable insights into the practical side of personnel planning, and his help in steering the project in the right direction. We also would like to thank the reviewers for their interest in the paper and their insightful comments.

References

[1] T. De Feyter and M.-A. Guerry, "Markov models in manpower planning: a review," 01 2011, pp. 67–88.

[2] V. O. Ezugwu and S. Ologun, "Markov Chain: A Predictive Model for Manpower Planning," Journal of Applied Sciences and Environmental Management, vol. 21 (3), 2017, pp. 557–565.

[3] B. A. Kassa and A. E. Tizazu, "Personnel scheduling using an integer programming model – an application at Avanti Blue-Nile Hotels," Springer Plus, 07 2013, online publication; doi: 10.1186/2193-1801-2-333; PMCID: PMC3923920, PMID: 24555163.

[4] Q. Chang, J. Ni, P. Bandyopadhyay, S. Biller, and G. Xiao, "Maintenance staffing management," vol. 18, 06 2007, pp. 351–360.

[5] B. Denkena, M. A. Dittrich, F. Winter, and C. Wagener, "Simulation-based planning and evaluation of personnel scheduling in knowledge-intensive production systems," Production Engineering: Research and Development, 10 2016, pp. 489–496.

[6] N. S. Narahari and K. N. Subramanya, "System dynamics modeling for human resource planning – a case study," URL: https://www.academia.edu/18935980/System_Dynamics_Modeling_For_Human_Resource_Planning_-_A_Case_Study [retrieved: August, 2018].

[7] "The Julia language," URL: https://julialang.org/ [retrieved: August, 2018].

[8] "SimJulia," URL: https://github.com/BenLauwens/SimJulia.jl [retrieved: August, 2018].

[9] "Julia Micro-Benchmarks," URL: https://julialang.org/benchmarks/ [retrieved: August, 2018].

[10] "SQLite," URL: https://www.sqlite.org/index.html [retrieved: August, 2018].

[11] "SQLite in Julia," URL: https://github.com/JuliaDatabases/SQLite.jl [retrieved: August, 2018].

[12] "yEd," URL: https://www.yworks.com/products/yed? [retrieved: August, 2018].

AMOSS: A Bespoke Stochastic Simulation Environment Built On Open Source Software

Edgar Whyte
Carl Sandrock
Greg Laycock
Deon Pretorius

Department of Chemical Engineering
University of Pretoria
Hatfield, GP 0028, South Africa
email: edgar.whyte@gmail.com
email: carl.sandrock@up.ac.za
email: gr3g.lk@gmail.com
email: u13160312@tuks.co.za

Gerrit Streicher

Group Technology
Sasol South Africa (Pty) Ltd
Sasolburg, FS 1947, South Africa
email:
gerrit.streicher@sasol.com

Jean-Pierre Cronje

Secunda Chemical Operations
Sasol South Africa (Pty) Ltd
Secunda, MP 2302, South Africa
email: jeanpierre.cronje@sasol.com

***Abstract*—Sasol's Operation Research department developed their own discrete event flow-sheet simulation methodology to Model Operations using Stochastic Simulation (MOSS). This generic methodology is not restricted to Sasol, but can be applied to any type of continuous process operation. In Sasol's case, MOSS has been so successfully applied that new process modifications will hardly be done without a MOSS simulation. However, these simulations require handling multi-component flows with material recycle as well as optimal allocation to units based on their capacity and profitability, resulting in complex models which require long development times. Commercial packages were evaluated to improve model development time using the MOSS methodology, but they did not comply with these requirements. Automatic Modelling Operations using Stochastic Simulation (AMOSS) is a bespoke simulation platform developed to fit the MOSS requirements using free/open source software. It is equation-oriented (as opposed to sequential modular) and automatically generates mass and component balance equations from user-generated process connectivity diagrams and operating unit specifications (reactor conversions, separator efficiencies and simulation-specific variables). It can allocate flows based on unit operating rules (unit priorities and capacities). Stochastic elements are introduced with user-defined distributions based on actual plant data.**

Keywords–stochastic simulation; Monte Carlo; flowsheeting; equation-orientated; equation ordering.

I. INTRODUCTION

Sasol is an integrated energy and chemicals industry in South Africa and leads the world in producing liquid fuels from natural gas and coal. The whole operation can be grouped into a number of value chains. A value chain normally consists of a group of interlinked plants, designed to produce a basic component which is then distributed and converted by consumer plants into value-added products, which are then supplied to their respective markets. The value chains and their external influences are studied and improved as a unit prevents the local optimization which results when only individual plants are optimized. Factors such as limited plant capacity, insufficient plant availability and sub-optimal operational philosophies are often the main constraints. A value chain can become quite complex when output streams are recycled back into the value chain. In such cases, a change can have a big impact on a completely different part of the operation, making it difficult for the plant Subject Matter Experts (SME) to envisage the impact and even harder to quantify the impact which is always required for the motivation of Capital Expenditure (CAPEX).

This is an example where process simulation can be applied with great effect. Since the model must be able to simulate plant availabilities, operational philosophies (rules and heuristics operators use to run the plant) and storage vessels, the model must be dynamic, stochastic and heuristic in nature. Over the years, Sasol has developed a modeling methodology, Modeling Operations using Stochastic Simulation (MOSS) [1], to determine the impact of modifications on value chains. The strength of such a simulation lies in the ability to quantify the impact of a change over the whole value chain and in the process reduce the amount of subjective decision-making. However, MOSS does not easily deal with value chains that have tightly coupled feedback loops where resource optimization is a prerequisite.

Before automation, the existing simulation method had to be extended by hand to simulate the operation with an acceptable level of accuracy. The modification included a number of complex mathematical formulae that had to be derived, programmed and tested. This added a significant amount of model development time, resulting in a delayed, but accurate set of results. This triggered the search for an alternative set of stochastic simulation tools.

A number of alternative software tools were identified, but due to time constraints, Sasol was not in a position to complete a proper study. Hence, the University of Pretoria was contracted to submit a modeling solution. The existing stochastic model [2], the existing optimization model and the existing steady state model were handed to the University as usable references.

The rest of this paper is organized as follows. Section II describes the performance criteria used to guide development. Section III discusses decisions made about the software development environment used to develop the simulation software. Section IV lists and explains the steps involved in developing a simulation using AMOSS. Section V elaborates on some of the steps to include information about the implementation. The conclusion summarizes the achievements of the project compared to the performance criteria and suggests future work.

II. Simulation Environment Requirements

Sasol proposed the following list of performance criteria for the new development environment. Note that the requirements are not completely independent. For example, an increase in accuracy can lead to an increase in development time.

Development time: The simulation environment must reduce development time compared to manual equation rewriting and not be affected by the complexity of the model.

Accuracy: The model must be appropriately accurate and the accuracy must be independent of the complexity of the value chain

Linear scalability: The resulting simulation must scale linearly with the number of units.

Development flexibility: New scenarios that require modification to the existing model must be easy and simple to incorporate.

Simulation time: The simulation execution time must be short which will ensure that sufficient replications per scenario can be run as well as more runs during model validation and verification. Target simulation time should be less than 3 minutes per replication consisting of 70000 time steps.

Package stability: The model must calculate a value for each variable in each time increment for all replications in all the scenarios.

Generic application: The solution must be able to model any value chain in Sasol irrespective of the combination and configuration of plants, which imply that the existing legacy models will be converted to the new modeling solution.

Debug capability: The solution must be able to guide the user to locate a bug in a faulty model and requires the recreation of an error situation in the same replication and scenario in which it had occurred.

Fit for purpose: The modeling environment must be focused on supporting the stochastic modeling methodology of the Sasol and allows for ability to add additional features and plants.

Learning curve: A quick learning curve is required for the model developer, but it is accepted that the learning curve for the software tool developer will take longer.

Version control: As more than one person can use the same model at any time, the solution must allow for simultaneous modification and development in a controlled manner.

Cause identification: When simulation results are counter-intuitive, the tool must allow the user to explain the results by relating causes and effects. The tool must also assist in finding bottlenecks.

Software Cost: Simulation packages are expensive and it will be difficult to justify purchasing a new simulation tool which will only partially solve Sasol's problem and therefore the initial cost as well as the annual maintenance cost must thus be low.

III. Software Development

The current Sasol value chain models that make use of the MOSS methodology are developed in MS Excel using VBA [3] but fail some of the simulation environment requirements mentioned. Most notably, the current solution requires manual rewriting of equations in order to satisfy continuity equations balances. Additionally, heuristics must be embedded in the simulation code manually in order to do optimal unit allocation.

Alternative simulation platforms, namely Simio [4] and AnyLogic [5] were investigated, but they did not allow for the simulation of continuous multi-component process streams with optimal allocation at each time step. Both packages have the ability to simulate continuous process flows and Simio has the ability to do splitting of streams to maximise throughput. The operating philosophies of the Sasol plant, however, call for more widespread optimisation at each time step than these packages supply without custom development.

AMOSS is built using mainly open-source tools. It is written in Python [6], the graphical flowsheeting is done in Open Modelica's Connection Editor OMEdit [7] while the Atom [8] text editor facilitates additional user inputs. Although not open source, Microsoft Excel [9] is widely available and used as an interface for editing tabular data.

The open source technologies allow for simple modifications to accommodate the needs of the platform.

IV. Modeling and Simulation Work-Flow

The basic work-flow of AMOSS is illustrated in Figure 1 and descriptions of the steps are as follows:

Step 1 requires the user to draw a process diagram in OMEdit together with operational unit-specific data in Excel. The unit library contains the unit operations of concern in the Sasol value chains (Buffers, Reactors, Pipes and Separators). User inputs such as a component list, flow rates, separator splits, buffer sizes and reactor conversions are entered during this step.

Step 2 takes the OMEdit diagram which contains the process connectivity and operational unit information and parses it into a network graph. Using graph theory, a graph table is generated containing the connectivity and attributes of the process units.

Step 3 iterates through the graph, creating all the necessary equations automatically. These equations are categorized as component mass balance equations, total flow equations, mix point equations, reactor equations, separator equations and buffer equations.

Step 4 tears the equations using the block lower triangular method and symbolically solves the smaller blocks to lower the stiffness of the system of equations, making it easier to solve. Prior to pre-solving equations, a degree of freedom (DOF) analysis is done to ensure that the system is not under- or over-specified.

Step 5 requires the user to define additional equations to describe how the unit is operated (operating rules) together with identifying which variables or parameters are stochastic and provide a distribution. These rules are typically the unit constraints (minimum and maximum capacities) of the units, as well as the feed distribution priority between multiple units receiving feed from the same source. The stochastic element's distributions are also specified by the user during this step.

Step 6 takes the system of equations in Step 4 and concatenates it with the equations in Step 5 and tears these equations, using the bordered block lower triangular method, producing the full system of equations. The bordered lower triangular form of the system of equations requires less variables to be solved simultaneously compared to the unordered system. A model is created from the ordered system and is solved using numerical root-finding software.

Step 7 simulates the process for all active scenarios for the number of required replications. Results generated are written to a file.

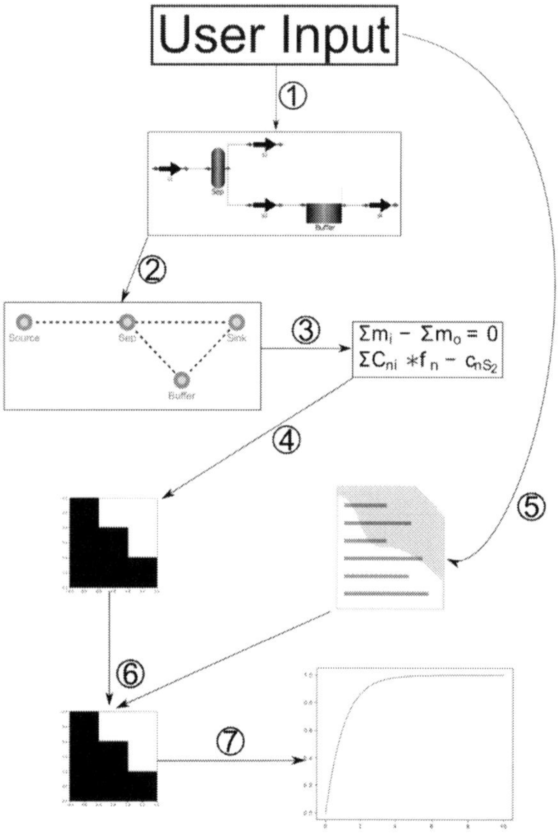

Figure 1. Illustration of AMOSS work-flow

V. Simulation Environment Components

To better understand the work-flow and the operation of AMOSS this section elaborates on some of the components. The work-flow starts with with a graphical description of the process model in flowsheet form. This flowsheet is then parsed and the equations implied by the connectivity are created, ordered and pre-solved. It is also possible to include additional equations which specify behaviour on the plant rather than the mass and energy balances attached to the units.

A. *Process flowsheet*

Figure 2 shows an example of a process diagram in OMEdit. The building blocks are dragged and dropped from a library of operations. The building blocks are as follows:

- **Source** is the location where mass enters the simulated process.
- **Sink** is the location where mass exits the simulated process.
- **Mix Point** is an operational unit where streams of different compositions are mixed and the streams leaving the Mix Point all have the same composition.
- **Buffer** is a tank or accumulator within the process.
- **Reactor** is an operational unit where components can be converted to different components.
- **Pipe** is a block used to give streams names and indicate the flow direction.
- **Separator** is the operational unit that models a distillation column. The block splits incoming streams into multiple streams with different compositions.
- **Visual Unit** is used to indicate a conglomeration of process operations, but acts as a Mix Point.

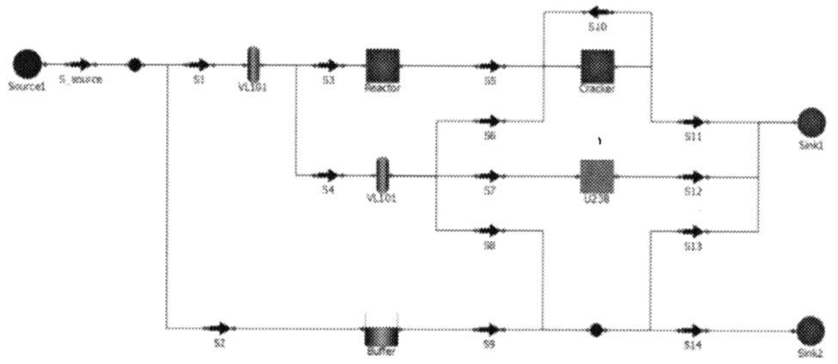

Figure 2. Example of the graphical process interface by utilizing OMEdit

The input data is required to yield a degree of freedom equal to zero. In each simulation, the component and total flow rates will be calculated. In Table I, inputs specific to Pipes S1 to Sn are listed.

TABLE I. Example table of component (left), stream and composition inputs (right).

Components	stream	comp
comp1	S1	total
comp2	S2	comp1
⋮	⋮	⋮
compn	Sn	compn

The number of rows required in the input table per Separator is equal to the number of Pipes connected to outlet minus one ($nP-1$). The number of columns in the table corresponds to the number of components plus two ($nC+2$). For example in row 1 of Table II, if S6_f1 is set to 0.5, 50% of the comp_1 mass flow entering the Separator will go to Pipe S6.

The number of rows in the input table per Reactor is equal to the number of components in the component list

TABLE II. EXAMPLE TABLE OF INFORMATION REQUIRED FOR EACH SEPARATOR.

node	attribute	comp_1	comp_2	···	comp_n
Separator	S6	S6_f1	S6_f2	⋱	⋮
Separator	Sx	Sx_f1	Sx_f2	⋮	⋮
VL101	S101	S101_f1	S101_f2	···	S101_fn

(nC). The number of columns in the table correspond to the number of components plus two ($nC + 2$). Column 1 contains the name of the Reactor and column 2 is the list of components entering the Reactor. The remaining column headings indicate the components exiting the Reactor. The table contains the conversion of each component entering the Reactor (comp_x in) to another component (comp_x out). For example R1_c1i_c2o (*Reactor1 comp_1 in comp_2 out*) is the fractional conversion of comp_1 to comp_2.

TABLE III. EXAMPLE TABLE OF INFORMATION REQUIRED FOR EACH REACTOR.

node	comp	comp_1 out	comp_2 out	···	comp_n out
Reactor	comp_1 in	R1_c1i_c1o	R1_c1i_c2o	···	R1_c1i_cno
Reactor	comp_2 in	R1_c2i_c1o	R1_c2i_c2o	⋱	⋮
Reactor	⋮	⋮	⋮		
Reactor	comp_n in	R1_cni_c1o	R1_cni_c2o	···	R1_cni_cno
Cracker1	comp_1 in			⋱	⋮
Cracker1	⋮				
Cracker1	comp_n in			···	R2_cni_cno

B. Automatic equation generation

With the connectivity specified, the conservation of mass and chemical reaction equations are automatically generated by the system. In the MOSS methodology, these equations would be written into code by hand. This represents a significant improvement in efficiency.

A directed graph is extracted from the process diagram and processed using NetworkX [10], a Python library with a variety of graph theory algorithms. All the operational units in the diagram are vertices and the pipes indicate the edges between vertices, together with edge direction.

The bipartite graph generated from the extracted information, is used to construct a directed graph (Figure 3). This is how the basic equations that describe the mass balance, mix point, component conversion, component split and integral equations for the buffers are created.

Next, the degrees of freedom are calculated to ensure that the system is correctly specified.

C. Pre-solving equations

Pre-solving refers to the analytical solving of the system of equations created in the previous section, prior to running the simulation. The intent is to speed up the simulation by avoiding numerical solving of equations.

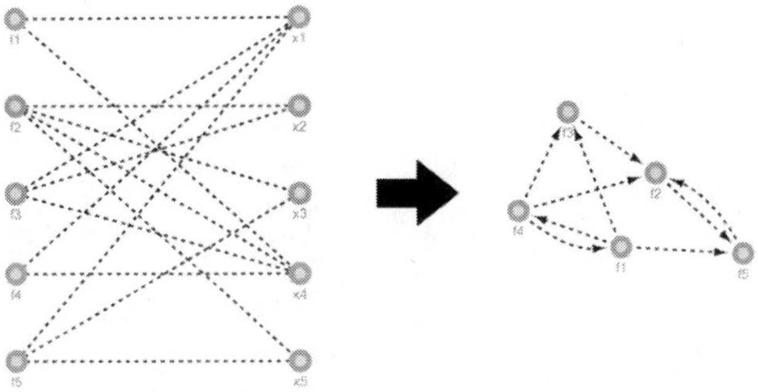

Figure 3. Directed graph created from the bipartite graph

Sympy [11] is used to convert all the equations to symbolic mathematical expressions. A tearing method is used to tear the system of equations into subsets of equations that require simultaneous solving. The tearing is achieved decomposition of the unordered incidence matrix (Equation 1) to a bordered lower triangular incidence matrix (Equation 2)

$$[A] = \begin{array}{c} \\ f_1 \\ f_2 \\ f_3 \\ f_4 \\ f_5 \end{array} \begin{array}{c} \begin{array}{ccccc} x_1 & x_2 & x_3 & x_4 & x_5 \end{array} \\ \begin{pmatrix} \textcircled{1} & & & 1 & \\ & 1 & 1 & 1 & \textcircled{1} \\ 1 & \textcircled{1} & & 1 & \\ 1 & & & \textcircled{1} & \\ 1 & & \textcircled{1} & & 1 \end{pmatrix} \end{array} \tag{1}$$

$$[A] = \begin{array}{c} \\ f_1 \\ f_2 \\ f_3 \\ f_4 \\ f_5 \end{array} \begin{array}{c} \begin{array}{ccccc} x_1 & x_2 & x_3 & x_4 & x_5 \end{array} \\ \begin{pmatrix} \textcircled{1} & 1 & & & \\ 1 & \textcircled{1} & & & \\ 1 & 1 & \textcircled{1} & & \\ 1 & & & \textcircled{1} & 1 \\ & 1 & 1 & 1 & \textcircled{1} \end{pmatrix} \end{array} \tag{2}$$

D. External user equations

AMOSS provides a platform to input additional equations to describe the process activities and operating instructions. In the MOSS methodology, it is common to distribute mass into different pipes based on minimum and maximum constraints, together with allocation priorities. If the constraints are local to the distribution point, the distribution is determined analytically. If the constraints are up- or downstream of the distribution point, general optimization is required.

These inputs are done using the Atom text editor with a customized script for syntax checking and tab completion (Figure 4).

The probability distributions are also specified as a table input, with the option to switch between discrete and continuous distributions:

Once the full system of equations are created, it is ordered to ease the solving effort. Figure 5 is an example of an incidence matrix using a test process of AMOSS with 171 variables and equations. The unordered state implies that 171 equations need to be solved simultaneously. Using the bordered lower triangular ordering algorithm of Baharev [12] on the system results in the ordered incidence matrix. In this form there are only 19 free variables, while the values of the remaining variables are solved by direct substitution.

TABLE IV. EXAMPLE OF HOW A USER CAN DEFINE A DISTRIBUTION.

Discrete	0
value	P
0	0
1	0.0625
2	0.125
3	0.1875
4	0.25
5	0.1875
6	0.125
7	0.0625
8	0

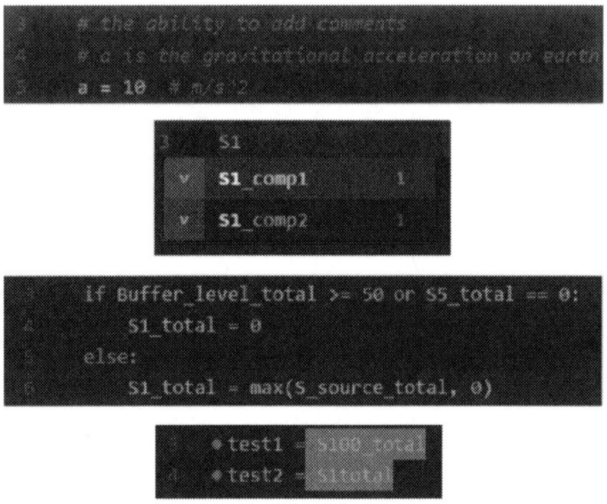

Figure 4. Entry of user inputs via Atom. From top to bottom: Adding comments, tab completion, syntax highlighting and error indication.

The model is built in CasADi [13]. The need for an algorithmic differentiation tool is required due to the optimization operations introduced by the distribution of material according to certain constraints. CasADi is also used to find the roots of the system of equations.

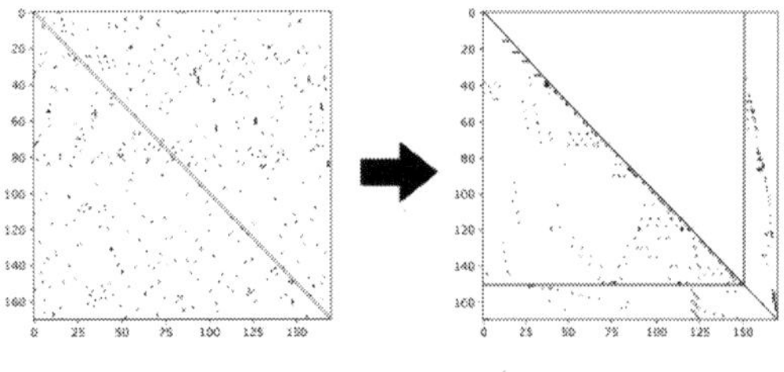

Figure 5. Unordered incidence matrix is ordered to bordered lower triangular form

VI. IMPROVEMENTS TO DATE

Most of the improvements that were attempted to date was to speed up the simulation time. The following simulation speed improvements have been attempted:

HDF5 The HDF5 file format was used to improve the performance of saving results to disk, because the format yields a file 15 times smaller than a CSV file. **BLT ordering** Block lower triangular ordering was used to increase the simulation speed. The improvement seen by implementing BLT tearing is due to the reduction in the number of variables that need to be solved numerically. **CasADi** The implementation of CasADi shows the power of derivative information. **Parallel Processing** The simulations of AMOSS are embarrassingly parallel (the scenarios can be simulated completely independently of one another). Celery [14] is used to distribute the load of the scenarios.

Figure 6 shows the effect of each of these improvements on the simulation time. Parallel processing scales all these times by a constant factor for each CPU used.

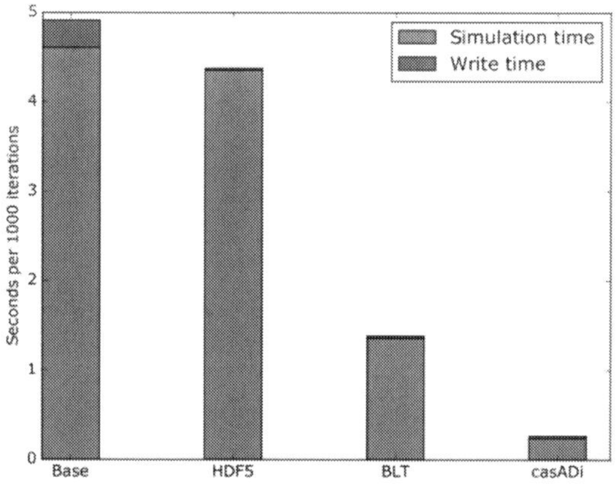

Figure 6. Simulation runtimes of the AMOSS test process with the cumulative improvements

VII. CONCLUSION

AMOSS successfully provides a stochastic simulation platform. AMOSS encompasses a variety of different aspects, such as automatic equation generation, equation ordering, optimization and parallel processing, to support this platform.

A. *Achieved requirements*

The deliverables that are satisfied by AMOSS are:

Reduction in development time The ability to generate equations automatically given a process diagram together with the equation ordering drastically reduces development time. In MOSS, equations are manually derived for systems that include recycles. When rebuilding a value chain in AMOSS, the Sasol user reported a 6 week saving in development time.

Generic application AMOSS was designed as a general stochastic simulation platform. The operational unit library can be easily expanded and the code downstream of the automatic equation generation will remain unchanged.

Development flexibility Changing the operating instructions or connectivity in the existing MOSS models requires major effort. The manually generated equations will require modification. Changing the model in AMOSS just requires changes to connectivity and operating instructions.

Simulation flexibility: AMOSS allows sections of the plant to be deactivated with logical operators in the operating instructions.

Acceptable accuracy: On condition that the Newton root finder successfully finds a solution under 1000 function evaluations, any residual equation will be solved with an absolute error of 10^{-12}.

Fit for purpose: AMOSS is an extension of the MOSS methodology and was developed with the guidance of Sasol and therefore follows the modelling methodology of Sasol. AMOSS is written in Python, which is a common language with a large community, making it possible for a person with moderate programming experience to contribute to AMOSS.

Linear scalability: AMOSS simulation time does scale linearly depending on the number of equations in the system, provided that the difficulty stays constant.

Quick learning curve: The Sasol user has reported the learning curve as low to moderate, requiring only 1 week to build a medium sized model. The most difficult part is to learn basic Python grammar and how to create an OpenModelica flowsheet together with rudimentary coding skills. This compares favourably to the skills required to solve the equations and code the model in the MOSS methodology.

Software cost: The software cost for AMOSS is low relative to other commercial software due to the use of open source software like Python and OpenModelica.

Version control: Version control of the project is done with Git using Bitbucket as the cloud repository. Since model files are plain text, it is also easy to track model development using Git.

B. Future work

Three of the deliverables of the AMOSS requirements could not be met. These are fast simulation time and software package stability.

Fast simulation time: When comparing a model built in AMOSS against the same model using the MOSS methodology in VBA, the VBA model speed is superior. The benchmark process takes 1.7 minutes to complete a replication of 70 128 hours, whereas AMOSS simulates the same process in 24 minutes. The leading cause is the high number of variables that needs to be solved numerically. A high number of these variables stem from infeasible assignments. Investigation into eliminating the infeasible assignments is required.

Software package stability: AMOSS is stable in the sense that is does not close unexpectedly, but the graphical user interface is considered unstable. Focus will be given to develop a more robust and user-friendly interface.

Cause identification: Rudimentary cause identification is added by identifying when a logical operator is evaluated as true. A list linking the created if-variables to the statement is made available to the modeler. This feature needs to be further developed to elicit better understanding of the simulation results.

REFERENCES

[1] M. Meyer, R. Hylton, M. Fisher, A. van der Merwe, G. Streicher, J. J. van Rensburg et al., "Innovative decision support in a petrochemical production environment," Interfaces, vol. 41, no. 1, 2011, pp. 79–92. [Online]. Available: http://www.jstor.org/stable/23016181

[2] G. Streicher, "A stochastic simulation model of a continuous value chain operation with feedback streams and optimization," in Proceedings of the 2013 Winter Simulation Conference: Simulation: Making Decisions in a Complex World, IEEE. Piscataway, New Jersey: IEEE Press, 2013, pp. 3912–3912.

[3] Microsoft, "Office vba language reference," https://msdn.microsoft.com/en-us/vba/vba-language-reference, 2018, (Accessed on 04/14/2018).

[4] Simio LLC, "Simulation, production planning and scheduling software — simio," https://www.simio.com/index.php, 2017, (Accessed on 04/27/2017).

[5] The AnyLogic Company, "Multimethod simulation software and solutions," http://www.anylogic.com/, 2017, (Accessed on 04/28/2017).

[6] Python Software Foundation, "Python software foundation," https://www.python.org/, 2018.

[7] OpenModelica, "Openmodelica connection editor (omedit) - openmodelica," https://openmodelica.org, 2017.

[8] GitHub Inc, "Atom," https://atom.io/, 2018.

[9] Microsoft, "Excel 2016 by microsoft - spreadsheet software," https://products.office.com/en-za/excel, 2018, (Accessed on 2018-04-14).

[10] N. developers, "Networkx," https://networkx.github.io/, October 2017, (Accessed on 04/14/2018).

[11] A. Meurer, C. P. Smith, M. Paprocki, O. Čertík, S. B. Kirpichev, M. Rocklin et al., "Sympy: symbolic computing in python," PeerJ Computer Science, vol. 3, Jan. 2017, p. e103. [Online]. Available: https://doi.org/10.7717/peerj-cs.103

[12] A. Baharev, "Exact and heuristic methods for tearing," https://sdopt-tearing.readthedocs.org/, November 2017, (Accessed on 04/14/2018).

[13] J. Andersson, "A general-purpose software framework for dynamic optimization," PhD thesis Arenberg Doctoral School, KU Leuven, Department of Electrical Engineering and Optimization in Engineering Center, October 2013.

[14] A. Solem et al, "Homepage - celery: Distributed task queue," http://www.celeryproject.org/, November 2017, (Accessed on 04/14/2018).

Development of Flexible and Lightweight Ballistic Body Armor

Constructional Contributions for Ballistic Components out of Ultra-High-Molecular-Weight Polyethylene

Henrik Seeber, Arash Ramezani
Chair of High-Speed Dynamics
Helmut Schmidt University - University of the Federal Armed Forces
Hamburg, Germany
Email: henrik.seeber@hsu-hh.de, ramezani@hsu-hh.de

Abstract—**In the last years, the risk to become a victim of a gun fight or to be involved into an amok situation increased. This leads to a higher demand for ballistic protection of civilians. Therefore, another capability profile for ballistic armor is necessary, compared to the military or police sector. The focal point of civil ballistic armor is wearing comfort, weight and invisibility. This paper provides information about the development of flexible and lightweight ballistic body armor. The manufacturing process is showed, heat- and sag test are presented, and first ballistic trials will be discussed below. The aim of the project is to create a ballistic body armor, which is flexible, and body fit enough to be worn under a sweater or suit. Furthermore, the body armor should meet the fourth level of ballistic protection of the "Association of test laboratories for bullet resistant materials and constructions" (VPAM 4). The idea can be realized by using an ultra-high molecular weight polyethylene (UHMWPE) composite. A material with well-balanced properties to fulfill the ballistic and mechanical requirements.**

Keywords - defense engineering; ballistic body armor; armor systems; fiber-reinforced plastics; ballistic trials; material processing.

I. Introduction

Personal integrity is a basic need. Nowadays, this need is endangered by increased incidents relating to gun violence. Especially in the USA, the number of incidents rises from about 50,000 to over 60,000 between 2014 and 2017 [1]. This leads to a higher need for personal ballistic protection at the civilian markets. Included are products like soft-ballistic sweater inlays or discrete ballistic vest, which are suitable for everyday life. In this area of use weight, wearing comfort and invisibility are focal points. The ballistic protection up to the fourth level of ballistic protection of the "Association of test laboratories for bullet resistant materials and constructions" (VPAM 4) has to be ensured. These requirements make it necessary to use a material, which combines high tensile strength for a high ballistic performance and low density for a suitable weight balance. These attributes are combined in many fiber reinforced composite materials, especially ultra-high molecular weight polyethylene (UHMWPE) is well suited for the mentioned application. Already existing analyses of the ballistic behavior of UHMWPE, like in [2] or [3] described, are often on a theoretical level. This paper aims for an analysis on an applied level, with a concrete connection to a product development. Existing theoretical results are applied to the development of an actual ballistic vest. This leads to the overall aim of the project to create a flexible and lightweight ballistic vest, which meet the VPAM 4 regulations and can be worn under everyday clothes. Therefore, the project is divided into five sections:

1. Material processing (Section IV);
2. Material pre-testing (Section V);
3. Pre-ballistic testing (Section VI);
4. Ballistic testing (future work);
5. Finalization (future work).

This paper aims to provide data to derive a decision about the material composition, which is used for the future work.

The paper is structured as follows. In Section II, preliminary considerations are introduced regarding material, processing and shape of the test objects. Section III gives a brief information about the used UHMWPE prepreg material and the second matrix material. Section IV is about the processing of ballistic plates namely cutting and lamination process. In Section V, heat resistance test and sag test are presented and discussed. In Section VI, the pre-ballistic test, which includes VPAM 3 (third level of ballistic protection of the "Association of test laboratories for bullet resistant materials and constructions") and VPAM 4 testing, is described and evaluated. The final section, Section VII, merge all results and, these results are discussed, leading to the constructive design of the plates.

II. Preliminary Considerations

In the beginning of the project two questions occur:

- Which material is suitable for the project (ballistic performance and weight)?
- How can it be processed to become a flexible ballistic plate?

First thoughts about the material leads to the UHMWPE in detail Dyneema® HB26. This material, in shape of hard-ballistic-plates, was successfully tested in previous ballistic trails. The plates were made out of multiple layer of pre-impregnated fiber (prepreg) material, which are fused under a certain pressure and temperature to become a solid ballistic plate. These ballistic trails have already been reported in [3].

This type of Dyneema® HB26 plates have an inflexible structure, making them unsuitable for this project of soft-ballistic-plates. On the other hand, the material shows a good ratio between weight and ballistic performance. In detail, areal density of the material is between 257 – 271 g/m² [3] and has an energy absorption per areal density of ~35 J·m²/kg [3]. In Section IIIA the mechanical properties of the material are explained in detail to enhance the awareness for the material.

Relating to the second initial question, Dyneema® HB26 provides a promising starting point, because this basic prepreg already offers a flexible structure. Therefore, the prepreg material only needs a second flexible matrix material to hold the prepreg layers together. Due to this, a lamination process by hand is selected, which makes it possible to use a flexible cast resin. This leads to the question, which kind of cast resin has to be used as a second matrix material. It has to be considered, that, firstly, the cast resin does not destroy the chemical basic structure of the prepreg material and secondly, the cast resin remains flexible. To ensure this chemical compatibility of the second matrix material the same matrix material, like it is used for the prepreg, is chosen. For that reason, a polyurethane (PUR) determines the second matrix material. This is selected out of the group of thermoplastic elastomers (TPE) [4]. Under the aspect of flexibility, a cast resin out of PUR with special flexible properties is chosen. A further description of the second matrix material is given in Section IIIB.

Beside the material, also the shape of the plates is important for the ballistic performance. This is, because of the anisotropic properties, which are described in Section IIIA. In this case, the shape was predetermined, because the plates have to fit into already existing structures.

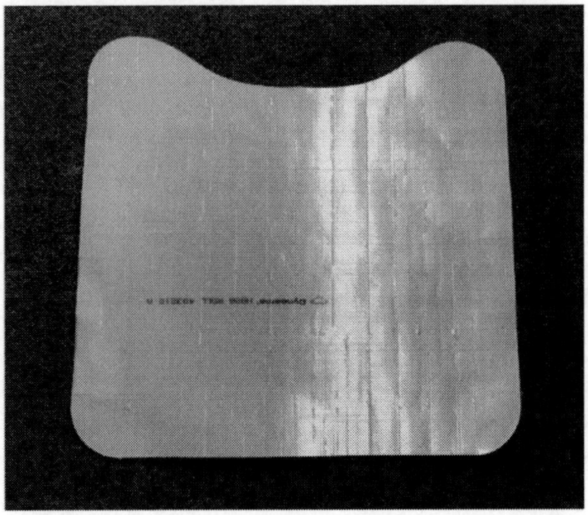

Figure 1. Main body pattern out of Dyneema® HB26. Width of 435 mm and a total height of 415 mm.

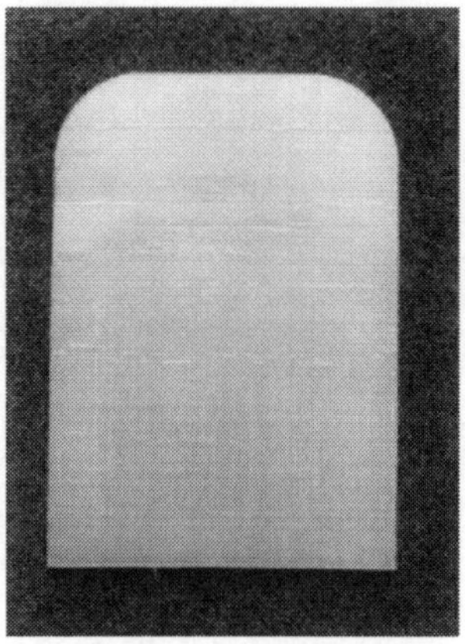

Figure 2. Side body pattern out of Dyneema® HB26. Width of 150 mm and a total height of 205 mm.

Relating to the standard size of a plate carrier inlay, plates were produced in a size of 300 mm x 250 mm. Furthermore, patterns for a sweatshirt inlay were used to evaluate the behavior of the different shapes in a ballistic trail. The main body pattern has a width of 435 mm and a total height of 415 mm (Figure 1). The side body pattern is narrower and has a width of 150 mm and a height of 205 mm (Figure 2).

III. USED MATERIALS

The basic material for the development of the flexible plates is Dyneema® HB26. It is shipped in a shape of a tape and as such, the matrix and fiber have already combined to a prepreg. The fiber is out of UHMWPE and the matrix out of PUR. As mentioned in Section II, the second matrix material is a flexible PUR.

A. Dyneema® HB26

The prepreg material consists of four sublayers of UHMWPE fibers, which are bidirectional orientated. The fiber direction per sublayer is turned by 90°, compared with the previous layer. This achieves an equal force dissipation in the prepreg material. Resulting from this structure, different geometric shapes of the material have anisotropic tensile properties, because of unequal fiber length.

The prepreg material has a density of 0.97 g/cm³. UHMWPE fibers have a high molecular weight. Commonly they have an Intrinsic Viscosity (IV) from 8 IV up to 30 IV. The fiber achieves high tensile strength (between 3.21 GPa and 5.99 GPa) and initial modulus (between 113GPa and 171 GPa) through long molecular chains out of methylene groups (CH_2). A characteristic of UHMWPE is, that the intra molecular bounds are relative weak Van der Waals bounds. Though, the extreme long molecule chains leading to a significant overlap between the molecule chains. This results in many inter molecular Van der Waals bounds, which strengthen the overall intermolecular stability. Further developments have to consider, that the fiber length is one of the most important constructional attributes, because of the link to the tensile strength of the material [5].

The matrix material of the prepreg has multiple tasks. Firstly, to protect the fiber against environmental conditions, pressure and kinks. Secondly, to hold the fibers in their position and direction. Finally, the matrix leads the forces into the fibers. Matrix material is often chosen from the group of thermoplastic elastomers, because of moldability and high elongation at break. These are good properties to support the fibers and the construction.

B. *Cast Resin System - Second Matrix Material*

The most important requirement for second matrix material is to preserve the flexibility of the prepreg. Therefore, the second matrix material has also to be flexible. As mentioned in Section II, the flexible PUR called R15GB-flex was selected. This material is a two-components cast resin system, consisting out of resin and hardener. With a mixing ratio of 100 parts resin and 25 parts hardener a Shore hardness (A) of ~40 is achievable. Compared with normal PUR cast resin systems, which have a Shore hardness (D) of ~65 (comparable to a Shore hardness (A) of ~105), the used PUR has a softer texture [6]. Another important property is the density of the second matrix material to keep a low overall weight. The material R15GB-flex has a density of 1.1 g/cm^3, comparable with the density of the prepreg material. The material has in mixed condition a medium viscosity and a processing time of approximately 15 min (100 g at 20 °C). These properties make the material suitable for the lamination process by hand. The maximum usage temperature is around 50 °C [5]. This fact will further be discussed in Section V.

IV. Processing

The processing of the ballistic plates is divided into two stages:

- Cutting process for semi-finished parts;
- Lamination process for the finished composite material.

A. *Cutting Process*

This project stage needs two patterns. First of all, the standard plate carrier inlay with rectangular, plane shape and dimensions of 300 mm x 250 mm. For the testing procedures one 5-layer, two 10-layer, one 15-layer and two 20-layer plates are produced (Table 1). Overall, 80 layers of prepreg material in this shape are necessary.

Furthermore, patterns for a sweatshirt inlay, with a main body part (Figure 1) and side part (Figure 2) are used. On the whole, 30 main body part layers and 15 side part layers are produced (Table I).

The lamination process by hand makes it necessary to laminate every single layer. In this particular case, a fast-laser-cutting-process is unsuitable, because the individual layers would melt together. A single layer cut with the laser cutter is as well inefficient, due to the rectangular shape. For that reason, every layer has to be cut out by a special scissor for reinforced fibers.

To achieve a high precision, the more complex shapes of the sweatshirt patterns are cut by the laser. The patterns are replicated in a computer-aided design (CAD) program and saved as drawing exchange format (DXF) file. Lastly, the file is exported into the laser cutter program and executed (parameters: Power 120 W, frequency 1000 Hz, velocity 0.036 m/s). Due to the four-sublayer structure of the prepreg material, a homogeneous sublayer structure is achievable even without rotation between the prepreg layers.

B. *Lamination Process*

The hand lamination process requires following stages:

- Mixing;
- Coating;
- Hardening process.

In the mixing process, the mixing ratio is adjusted by the proportion of weight. For a low Shore hardness (A) the manufacturer recommends a mixing ratio of 100 parts resin and 25 parts hardener. Proportion of weight of the two components, which is necessary for the different plate sizes, are shown in Table II. The two components are mixed with a wooden stick to a homogenous mixture.

This mixture is equal spread over the prepreg layer with a lamination brush. For the coating, a slight film is sufficient. Pressure from the inside to the outside is applied to get a compact compound.

Finally, surplus material is removed, and the plates are laid into a warm place for 24 h for hardening. After the hardening process, the plates are inherently stable.

V. Heat and Sag Test

Besides the ballistic performance, further two primary material attributes of the new composite material have to be tested. Firstly, the heat stability in a heat test, because of possible high surface temperatures in area of use. Secondly, the flexibility of the material, as key functionality in a sag test.

A. *Heat Test*

Heat is a weak point of the second matrix material, due to its thermoplastic properties. Maximum temperature of usage is around 50 °C according to the manufacturer. Analyses of the possible area of use show, that the average temperatures are moderate temperatures between 10 °C and 30 °C, which are unproblematic for the composite material. Nevertheless, in desert areas, which are possible areas of use, surface temperatures can reach a maximum around 70 °C and daily surface temperatures around 60 °C [7]. To test the heat resistance of the composite material, one plate is faced a heat test.

TABLE I. Proportion of Weight of Resin and Hardener for Different Amount of Layers

Layer	Resin [g]	Hardener [g]	Final Thickness [mm]
5	42.6	11.55	2
10	85.2	23.1	4.2
15	127.8	34.65	6.8
20	170.4	6.2	9.3

TABLE II. OVERVIEW OF THE CONSTRUCTED TEST OBJECTS

Plate Number	Test Number	Layers	Thickness [mm]	Weight [g]	Shape	Processing Method
1	1	10	4	295.8	Rectangular	Lamination
2	2	10	4.2	295.9	Rectangular	Lamination
3	3	15	6.8	448.3	Rectangular	Lamination
4	4	20	9.2	614.8	Rectangular	Lamination
5	5M 5R	20	9	592.6	Rectangular	Lamination
6	/	5	2	159	Rectangular	Lamination
7	7	15	10	/	Side Part	Loose
8	8	10	6.4	/	Main Body Part	Loose
9	9	20	13.3	/	Main Body Part	Loose

The heat test proceeds as follows: an oven is preheated to a temperature of 30 °C. This 30 °C stage is used as a reference result. Every 30 min the temperature is set to a new value, first 50 °C, then 60 °C and finally 70 °C. The plate is left in the oven for 30 min. After 15 min and 30 min the plate is taken out and checked regarding: degeneration, flexibility, slip of layers and defects. A 5-layer plate (Plate No. 6) is chosen to ensure an even temperature distribution in material. Results are displayed in Table III.

The results show that the composite material, and especially the second matrix material withstand temperatures up to 50 °C without any property changes. At higher temperatures above 50 °C an increased flexibility is recognizable. After 30 min at 70 °C the layers of prepreg are movable 3 mm against each other. After this movement, the layers go back to their initial state. At all temperature stages the plate shows no degeneration and defects. Following a cooling phase, the second matrix material solidified again. Summing up, the higher temperatures are uncritical to the composite material.

TABLE III. RESULTS OF THE HEAT TEST

Tempe-rature [°C]	Time [min]	Degene-ration	Flexibility	Slip of Layers [mm]	Defects
30	15	Non	Unchanged	Non	Non
	30	Non	Unchanged	Non	Non
50	15	Non	Unchanged	Non	Non
	30	Non	Unchanged	Non	Non
60	15	Non	Slightly increased	Non	Non
	30	Non	Slightly increased	Non	Non
70	15	Non	Increased	>1	Non
	30	Non	Increased	3	Non

B. Sag Test

Flexibility is a key attribute of the used type of ballistic protection. Comparative values of the plate flexibility can be generated through a sag test. The aim of this test is to measure the sag of the plate under a certain load.

Therefore, a test procedure is created. The test setup is shown in Figure 3. The plates are laid onto two bars with a contact area of 10 mm x 250 mm on both sides. Moreover, the basic test setup consists of two rulers and a wooden baseplate (35 mm x 145mm), which are arranged as in Figure 3 shown. The sag test was conducted at 22 °C.
As a result of this arrangement, a basic load of 72.8 g lays up on the plate. Additionally, a 500 g block is used as a test weight. The center of the wooden baseplate is positioned in the middle of the plate at 150 mm x 125 mm. One ruler is placed for measurements and the other as an indicator for it. The zero height is 120 mm.

First, the initial height of the plate is measured. In this phase the plate has an additional load of 72.8 g. After 30 sec under these conditions, the height is measured.

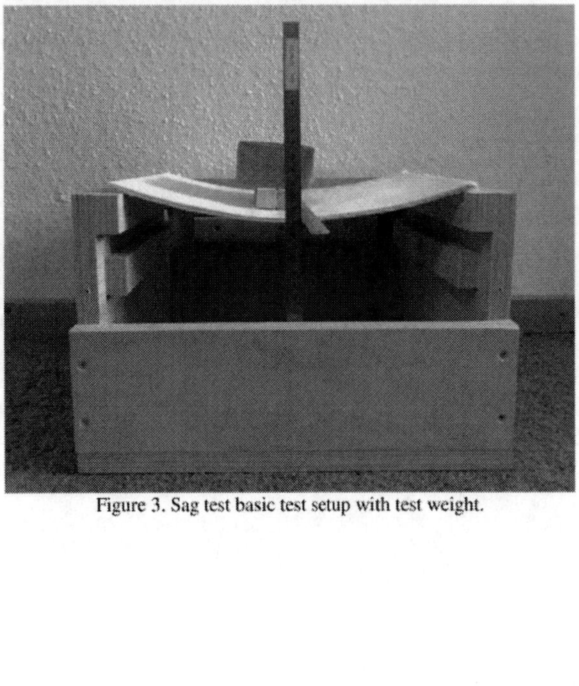

Figure 3. Sag test basic test setup with test weight.

TABLE IV. RESULTS OF THE SAG TEST

Plate Number	Initial Height [mm]	End Height [mm]	Delta (Sag) [mm]
1	131	165	34
2	143	183	40
3	129	153	24
4	123	128	5
5	125	128	3

Subsequently, the plate is loaded with test weight. After 10 sec under these conditions, the height is measured again. Results are displayed in Table IV. The results show that 20-layer plates have deficits in their sag values and thus in the overall flexibility. They may be too inflexible for this particular application area. The 15-layer plate has a good ratio between number of layers and flexibility, compared with the 10-layer plate.

VI. BALLISTIC TEST

The ballistic test is performed on the basis of the VPAM ("Association of test laboratories for bullet resistant materials and constructions") regulations. Especially following regulations are regarded: general basis for ballistic material, construction and product testing (APR) [8], ballistic protective vests (BSW) [9] and bullet resistant plate materials (PM) [10].

The aim of this project is to meet the regulations of VPAM 4. This level requires, that the plate withstand a penetration of a .357 Mag. fired with a projectile velocity of 430 ± 10 m/s from 5 m distance [8]. A ballistic placement test provides an overview of the ballistic performance of the composite material. Therefore, a modified VPAM 3 (9 mm, 415 ± 10 m/s, 5m) and VPAM 4 level is tested. The shooting distance is increased to 10 m. Penetration and back face deformation are evaluated. Based on VPAM BSW No. 4.2 a maximal transmitted energy of 70 J is acceptable.

A. Preparation and Test Setup

Two components are necessary for the test setup: shooting-box and plasticine (Figure 4). The shooting box is built in consideration of the VPAM BSW [9]. The inner dimensions of the shooting-box are 300 mm width, 250 mm height and 150 mm depth. Especially the characteristic depth is important, because of compression effects with the rear panel. Based on the VPAM PM contact areas of 30 mm on three sides are built in [9]. The used plasticine is recommended by VPAM (VPAM BSW No. 5.2) [9]. The ballistic test is conducted at an ambient temperature of 21 °C.

A measurement of the plasticity is conducted as described in VPAM BSW No. 5.2.1. The mean imprint depth (d_m) of the plasticine is 19.8 mm. With this value and the maximal transmitted energy (E_{max}) of 70 J, the maximal volume (V_{max}) of the back-face deformation is calculated as follows [8]:

$$V_{max} = (0.134 \cdot d_m - 1.13) \cdot E_{max} \quad (1)$$

$$V_{max} = (0.134 \cdot 19.8 - 1.13) \cdot 70 = 106.624 \quad (2)$$

Figure 4. Shooting-box filled with plasticine. Inner dimensions: 250 mm x 300 mm x 15 mm.

Figure 5. Left side: .357 Mag 158 Gr. Right side: 9 mm Luger 124 Gr.

This leads to a maximal back face deformation volume of 106.624 cm^3.

The gun, which is used for VPAM 3 testing is a SIG Sauer X-Five® with a 9 mm Luger 124 Gr. projectile. For the VPAM 4 testing an S&W 686 European Match® with a .357 Mag 158 Gr. projectile is used (Figure 5).

All shots are fired into the middle of the plates. The only exception is test number 5R, which get shot into the edge area. This edge shot has to hit the material in a distance of 30 ± 5 mm from an edge [9]. Test number 8 and 9 were shot without the shooting-box to check the penetration level of the loose layers.

B. Evaluation

After every shot the diameter and the depth of the imprint of the back-face deformation is measured (Table V). With these values, and the volume equation of a circular cone the volume of the back-face deformation (V) is calculated. Additionally, the transmitted energy (E) is calculated backwards with following equation [8]:

$$E = V / (0.134 \cdot d_m - 1.13). \quad (3)$$

TABLE V. RESULTS OF THE BALLISTIC TEST

Test Number	Layers	Caliber	Imprint -			Transmitted Energy [J]	Comments
			Depth [mm]	*Diameter [mm]*	*Volume [cm³]*		
1	10	9 mm	34.4	8.0	57.638	37.840	/
2	10	.357	/	/	/	/	Penetration
3	15	9 mm	26.0	7.0	33.353	21.897	/
4	20	.357	29.8	9.0	63.193	41.487	/
5M	20	9 mm	18.3	5.0	11.977	7.863	/
5R	20	9 mm	/	/	/	/	Leaving material
7	15	9 mm	40.4	7.0	51.698	33.940	/
8	10	9 mm	/	/	/	/	Stuck in fourth layer
9	20	.357	/	/	/	/	Stuck in fourth layer

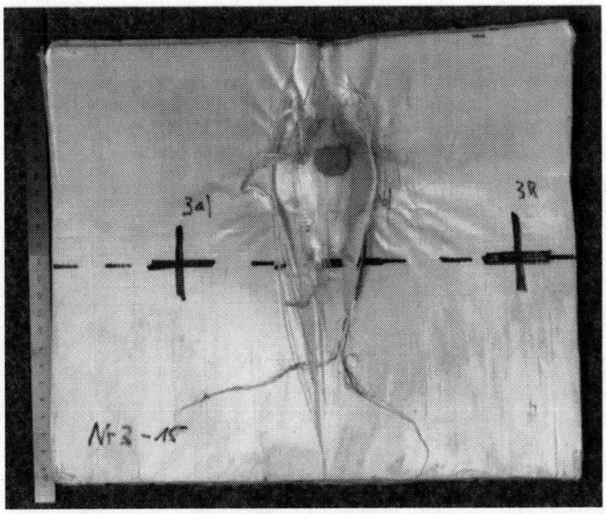

Figure 6. Test number 3 after the shot. Seeable is the back-face deformation and material behavior.

The results show, that test number 1, 3, 4, 5M, and 7 meet the requirement, that the transmitted energy is lower than 70 J. Especially test number three (15 layers) (Figure 6) shows a good average transmitted energy, comparing to test number 1 (10-layers) and 5M (20 layers).

Test number 5R failed, because the projectile left the plate before it gets stuck in the plate. As expected, test number 2 got penetrated by the .357 Mag projectile. This test was conducted to see the penetration behavior of the material and projectile, like layer and projectile movement, deformation of the projectile and damage to the plate. At test number 8 and nine the projectile got stuck in the fourth layer of the loose layers. The back-face deformation of these test numbers is negligible.

VII. DISCUSSION

The heat-resistance-test shows, that the composite plates are durable up to 70 °C. At higher temperatures a slip of layers is highly possible. Up to 60 °C no degeneration or melting is detectable (Table III). Thus, the second matrix material and main material are suitable for the estimated conditions.

To examine the flexibility, a sag test is conducted. It shows, that 20-layer plates are too stiff for this area of use. 10- and 15-layers plates show good values of flexibility and weight compared to other soft ballistic plates (Table IV).

The ballistic plate has to meet the requirements of VPAM 3 and VPAM 4. This requirement allows a maximal transmitted energy of 70 J. In a first placement test all expected plates meets this requirement by far (Table V). Also, the sweatshirt inlays were tested successfully. It seems, that the extensive shape, which leads to longer fibers, increases the ballistic performance.

To summarize, the 15-layer plate is the best performing plate, because of the ratio between flexibility, weight and ballistic performance. 10-layer plates will not meet the VPAM 4 regulations, and 20-layer plates are too stiff and heavy for the area of use. These results will put the 15-layer plate into the focus of the studies. It has to be considered, that these ballistic results are from a pre-testing series. They are just indicators for a relative rating between our ballistic plats. In further ballistic tests they have to be verified for the VPAM 4 level.

VIII. CONCLUSION AND FUTURE WORK

All in all, the aim of this project is to create lightweight and flexible ballistic body armor for the civilian market. Therefore, a UHMWPE prepreg as main material and a two-component flexible resin as second matrix material is used. Through a lamination by hand procedure, ballistic composite plates are produced. Because of this method, the flexible properties of the main material are sustained. Moreover, a temperature resistance of the composite material up to 60 °C is identified. All conducted experiments show, that the 15-layer plate full fill our expectations best. Especially, the ballistic results of this plate are promising. Furthermore, compared to other available products on the market, the new plate has a reduced weight of ~100 g, is 1.2 mm slimmer and full flexible.

In further scientific work, the 15-layer plate will be extensive ballistic tested. Especially, VPAM 4 testing will be focused. Greater effort will be spent into ballistic testing of the sweatshirt patterns and analyses of size-effects. Therefore, these special shaped plates will be also produced with the lamination process by hand and ballistic tested. Furthermore, new available prepreg material out of UHMWPE, special made for flexible ballistic plates, will be tested within following projects.

REFERENCES

[1] Gun Violence Archive, "Past Summary Ledgers", [Online]. Available from: http://www.gunviolencearchive.org/past-tolls [09.2018].

[2] L.H. Nguyen, "The Ballistic Performance of Thick Ultra High Molecular Weight Polyethylene Composite". RMIT University, Dec. 2015.

[3] H.v.d. Werff and U. Heisserer, "High performance ballistic fibers: Ultra-High Molecular Weight Polyethylene (UHMWPE)" in "Advanced Fibrous Composite Materials for Ballistic Protection", First Edition. Woodhead, Oct.2016.

[4] DSM Dyneema, "Product Specification Sheet HB26", Feb. 2014.

[5] T. Tam and A. Bhatnagar, "High-performance ballistic fibers and tapes" in "Lightweight Ballistic Composites: Military and Law-Enforcement", Second Edition. Amsterdam: Elsevier, May.2016.

[6] HP-Textiles, "HP-R15GB-flex Data Sheet", Aug. 2017.

[7] EOSDIS Worldview, "Land Surface Temperature (Day)" [Online]. Available from: https://go.nasa.gov/2P3DxzW [09.2018].

[8] Association of test laboratories for bullet resistant materials and constructions (VPAM), "VPAM APR 2006 Version 2", Nov. 2014.

[9] Association of test laboratories for bullet resistant materials and constructions (VPAM), "VPAM BSW 2006", May. 2009.

[10] Association of test laboratories for bullet resistant materials and constructions (VPAM), "VPAM PM 2007 Version 2", Jan. 2014.

Improved FSI Method for Blast Simulations

Arash Ramezani, Daniel Huber, Hendrik Rothe
Chair of Short-Time Dynamics
University of the Federal Armed Forces
Hamburg, Germany
Email: ramezani@hsu-hh.de, daniel.m.huber@hsu-hh.de, rothe@hsu-hh.de

Abstract—**The present time is shaped by a variety of religious, political and military conflicts. In times of asymmetric warfare and constantly changing sources of danger from terrorist attacks and other violence based crimes, the personal need for protection continues to rise. Aside from military applications, there is a large area for the use of high security vehicles. Outwardly almost indistinguishable from the basic vehicles, security vehicles are used for protecting heads of state, as well as individuals. To remain state of the art it is necessary for security vehicles to permanently continue to develop protection against modern weapons and ammunition types. It is enormously cost intensive to check any new technology by firing or blasting of real vehicles. Therefore, more and more calculations of new security concepts and materials are carried out by numerical computer simulations. However, product simulation is often being performed by engineering groups using niche simulation tools from different vendors to simulate various design attributes. The use of multiple vendor software products creates inefficiencies and increases costs. This paper will present the analysis and development of an interface between the most common Computer Aided Engineering (CAE) applications ANSYS Autodyn and Abaqus to exploit the advantages of both systems for the simulation of blast effects.**

Keywords-CFD-FEM coupling methods; fully automatic structure analysis; high-performance computing techniques; blast loading; vehicle structures.

I. INTRODUCTION

Since the 1960's, the simulation of physical processes has been a steadily growing and integral part of CAE. Especially, the Computational Fluid Dynamics (CFD) and the discretization of complex models using the Finite Element Method (FEM) have made an impressive development from individual highly specialized applications to the standard of industrial product development. This process was supported by the progressive development of increasingly powerful and less expensive computer hardware. Together with specialized software, a triumph of the simulation of physical processes in everyday technical work has emerged. Positive effects due to the use of simulation tools have been shorter development times, lower production costs, more innovative products, improved security and higher quality. The previous modelling of components and objects of the real world by Computer Aided Design (CAD) software is an important prerequisite for the efficient use of the simulation tools. This has been established as a standard in the automotive industry, so that almost every part of a vehicle can be constructed by using CAD. These complete and realistic vehicle models can be analyzed virtually by available simulation software.

The two leading software providers for CFD / FEM calculations are ANSYS (Canonsburg, USA) and Abaqus FEA from Dassault Systèmes (Vélizy-Villacoublay, France). Although both providers offer software with similar features available, their performance is characterized by different spreads and focuses. For example, Abaqus and CATIA, a CAD software, which is also distributed by Dassault Systèmes, is predominantly used by the automotive industry and provides excellent opportunities for the simulation and modelling of complete vehicles. This includes screwed and adhesive connections. On the other hand, ANSYS offers a wide range of sophisticated simulation capabilities in the field of CFD, which includes the modelling and simulation of explosive detonations and the subsequent propagation of shock waves. The different focuses of the performance of ANSYS and Abaqus yield to a mixed, demand-based use of the software in the research and development area, so that different software is used even within the same company on the same project in different areas of activity. This circumstance is amplified by the fact that product simulations are performed by engineering groups using niche simulation tools from different vendors to simulate various design attributes. Unfortunately, the leading software providers avoid the effective interaction of their simulation tools due to mutual competition. This complicates the development effort and results in longer development times in research and industry.

Particularly, in the area of armored security vehicles, it is necessary to remain state of the art and to constantly consider the ongoing development of modern weapon and ammunition types. Experimental tests of the harmful effects of new technologies by blast or impact is associated with enormous time and financial costs.

In order to exploit the full potential of ANSYS and Abaqus, we have developed an interface between these two software platforms [1]. This interface allows an iterative transfer of the blast simulation of ANSYS to the structural mechanic solver of Abaqus, which simulates the effects on the vehicle model and vice versa.

This paper reports on the development of this interface between ANSYS and Abaqus, which will enable combining the strengths of the two leading software providers with the aim of generating synergies that result in short development times and lower costs.

After a brief introduction and description of the different methods of space discretization in Section III, there is a short section on ballistic trials where the experimental set-up is depicted, followed by Section V describing the analysis with numerical simulations. The paper ends with a concluding paragraph in Section VI.

II. STATE-OF-THE-ART

A first step in developing an interface between ANSYS and Abaqus has already been reported in [1]. The developed interface allows accessing a set of data and passing them to Abaqus. Python was used as a programming language. ANSYS provides the data records for the interface as .txt files. These files contain data points with Cartesian coordinates, which describe the propagation of shock waves after blasting. The interface takes this data and splits it into separate information. In a further step, the data is stored in a list, linked with the corresponding time points, pressure data and coordinates. It is also possible to use a set of data and to interpolate between the time points to produce a larger data set. After the data has been written and saved in a linked form, the interface retrieves the CAD model. Subsequently, the explosion data can be projected onto a selectable surface of the model. Then, an iterative loop realizes the coupling between CFD and FEM simulations. This approach for a coupled CFD-FEM analysis is called "strong coupling." In another approach, the "semi-strong coupling," a smaller amount of data is used and mathematically interpolated for a sufficient approximation. The third concept is a "weak coupling" solution. Here, neural networks and deep learning can be used to replicate blast effects on different vehicle structures. Until now, the basic functionality of the interface could be validated on different models, including the model of a safety vehicle.

III. FUNDAMENTALS OF SIMULATION

In the security sector, the partly insufficient safety of people and equipment due to failure of industrial components are ongoing problems that cause great concern. Since computers and software have spread into all fields of industry, extensive efforts are currently being made in order to improve the safety by applying certain computer-based solutions. To deal with problems involving the release of a large amount of energy over a very short period of time, e.g., explosions and impacts, there are three approaches, which are discussed in [2].

As the problems are highly non-linear and require information regarding material behavior at ultra-high loading rates, which are generally not available, most of the work is experimental and may cause tremendous expenses. Analytical approaches are possible if the geometries involved are relatively simple and if the loading can be described through boundary conditions, initial conditions, or a combination of the two. Numerical solutions are far more general in scope and remove any difficulties associated with geometry [3].

For structures under shock and impact loading, numerical simulations have proven to be extremely useful. They provide a rapid and less expensive way to evaluate new design ideas. Numerical simulations can supply quantitative and accurate details of stress, strain, and deformation fields that would be very expensive or difficult to reproduce experimentally. In these numerical simulations, the partial differential equations governing the basic physical principles of conservation of mass, momentum, and energy are employed. The equations to be solved are time-dependent and nonlinear in nature. These equations, together with constitutive models describing material behavior and a set of initial and boundary conditions, define the complete system for shock and impact simulations.

The governing partial differential equations need to be solved in both time and space domains. The solution over the time domain can be achieved by an explicit method. In the explicit method, the solution at a given point in time is expressed as a function of the system variables and parameters, with no requirements for stiffness and mass matrices. Thus, the computing time at each time step is short but may require numerous time steps for a complete solution. The solution for the space domain can be obtained utilizing different spatial discretization, such as Lagrange [4], Euler [5], Arbitrary Lagrange Euler (ALE) [6], or mesh free methods [7]. Each of these techniques has its unique capabilities, but also limitations. Usually, there is not a single technique that can cope with all the regimes of a problem [8]. The crucial factor is the grid that causes different outcomes. Details are discussed in Section IV.

Due to the fact that all engineering simulations are based on geometry to represent the design, the target and all its components are simulated as CAD models. Real-world engineering commonly involves the analysis and design of complicated geometry. These types of analysis depend critically on having a modeling tool with a robust geometry import capability in conjunction with advanced, easy-to-use mesh generation algorithms [9]. It often is necessary to combine different simulation and modeling techniques from various CAE applications. However, this fact can lead to major difficulties, especially in terms of data loss and computational effort. Particularly the leading software providers prevent an interaction of their tools with competing products. But to analyze blast loading and its effects on vehicle structures, different CAE tools are needed. Therefore, it is important that an interface is provided that allows a robust interaction between various applications. Using a CAD neutral environment that supports direct, bidirectional and associative interfaces with CAE systems, the geometry can be optimized successively and analysis can be performed without loss of data [10].

IV. MATERIALS AND METHODS

Various approaches are possible when it comes to solving problems that involve the release of large amounts of energy in very short periods of time, which then propagate as shock waves or act as impact on structures. Analytical solutions offer a very powerful way to describe such a process. Unfortunately, their applicability is restricted to problems with simple geometries and few boundary and initial conditions. In contrast, numerical simulations offer much more general applications with complex structures and feasible solutions.

The underlying physical model of numerical simulations is provided by physical conservation laws, the equation of state and the constitutive model. Partial differential equations for the conservation of energy, momentum, and mass form the physical conservation laws. Furthermore, the equation of state combines the internal energy or temperature and the density or volume of a material with the pressure. As a result, changes in the density and irreversible thermodynamic processes such as shock-like heating can be considered. In addition, the constitutive model includes the influence of the material to be simulated and describes the effect of deformation, i.e. changes in shape and material strength properties.

Together, these equations form a set of coupled, time- and location-dependent, highly non-linear equations, which can be solved by computer calculations. The governing partial differential equations need to be solved in both time and space domains. The solution over the time domain can be obtained by an explicit method, which is an iterative method and leads to a step by step solution in the time domain. Software for numerical simulation of shock and impact processes is called a hydrocode [11].

A. *Methods of Space Discretization*

All existing structural dynamics and wave propagation codes obtain solutions to the Differential Equations (DEs) governing the field by solving an analogous set of algebraic equations. The governing DEs are not solved directly, because currently only a handful of closed-form solutions for DEs are available. The equations of structural dynamics, being a coupled set of rate equations, which account for the effects of severe gradients in stress, strain and deformation, material behavior ranging from solid to fluid to gas, temperatures from room temperature to melt temperature are highly nonlinear and do not lend themselves to closed-form solutions in the general case.

To get a solution over the spatial domain a discretization of the material with a mesh is necessary. FEM uses such a discretization by dividing the problem space into separate elements. These elements can have different shapes: In two dimensions, the shape of quadrilaterals or triangles, in three dimensions, hexahedrons and tetrahedrons are usually used. Even complicated geometries can be formed with these elements. Each FEM element has a certain number of nodes, which are located at its corners and have known spatial coordinates. The displacement of these nodes represents the unknowns of the partial differential equations to be solved. There are multiple, different spatial discretization methods related to FEM, such as Lagrange, Euler, ALE or mesh free methods. Each of these methods can be used independently, but some specific problems need a combination of different discretization methods.

1) Lagrange

The Lagrange method divides an object into a spatial grid where the grid is fixed to the object and moves with it. The material components within an element do not change. If forces are acting on a node, it is displaced, and thus the forces are transmitted to its neighboring nodes, similar to a spring-mass system. This results in deformations of the grid. The nodes of the edge elements of an object remain unchanged so that the boundary and interface conditions can be easily applied. Clear material boundaries are also available so that space outside the material does not require an extra grid and therefore the conservation of mass is automatically satisfied. Figure 1 shows two objects with its mesh as an example of the Lagrange method. Two objects consisting of different materials represented by the colors blue and green before (left side) and after impact (right side). The green object has an initial velocity in the direction of the blue object. The right side of the figure shows the discretization dependent deformation after the impact with the Lagrange solver. The mesh is bound to the objects and divides them into multiple elements. After an impact the objects deform due to the deformation of the elements. A weak point of the Lagrange method is a strong distortion of the mesh in heavily loaded regions, as shown in Figure 1. in the area adjacent to the green and blue object. In general, the Lagrange method is best suited for complex geometries and structures, projectiles and other solids. A disadvantage of Lagrange is the occurrence of strong distortions of mesh element at high loads. Such a distorted element can adversely affect the temporal solution of the simulation since the time step is proportional to the size of the smallest element.

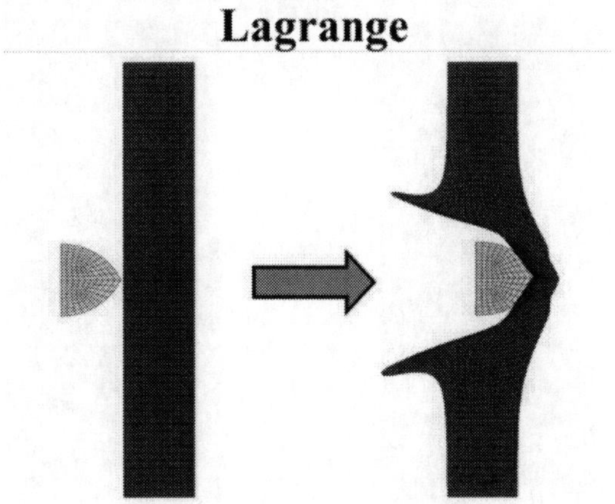

Figure 1. Lagrange method example.

In general, the Lagrange method is best suited for complex geometries and structures, projectiles and other solids. A disadvantage of Lagrange is the occurrence of strong distortions of mesh element at high loads. Such a distorted element can adversely affect the temporal solution of the simulation since the time step is proportional to the size of the smallest element.

2) Euler

In the Euler method, the coordinates of the nodes are fixed and form the entire mesh of the region to be solved. The material flows through the mesh as a function of time and changes the value of the element, while the spatial coordinates and the nodes remain fixed. This is the reason why no element distortion is possible in the Euler method. In contrast to Lagrange, boundary nodes do not necessarily coincide together with material boundary conditions. Thereby difficulties can arise with the application of boundary and interface conditions. Figure 2. shows two objects and the mesh as an example of the Euler method. Two objects consisting of different materials represented by the colors blue and green before (left side) and after impact (right side). The mesh fills the whole space. The green object has an initial velocity in the direction of the blue object. The right side of the figure shows the discretization dependent deformation after the impact with the Euler solver. The mesh is not bound to the objects like in the Lagrange frame. Instead the mesh fills the whole space with the objects and empty space between them. During the simulation, the material of the objects is transported through the mesh of the space. After an impact the mesh stays clear but its content is partly deformed.

In general, the Euler method is used to model the propagation of gases and fluids as a result of an explosion or impact. In the investigation of solids, the Euler method has a disadvantageous effect, since additional calculations are needed to transport the stress tensor and the history of the material through the lattice. In this case Euler needs more computing performance and smaller elements to resolve the occurring shock waves.

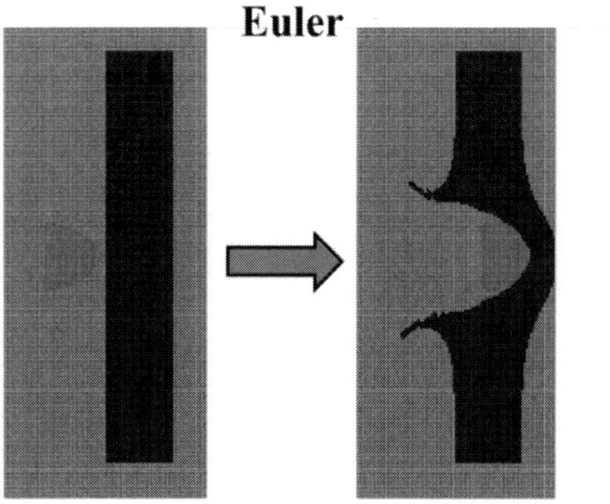

Figure 2. Euler method example.

3) ALE

The ALE method is a mix of Lagrange and Euler method. ALE allows an arbitrary redefinition of the mesh on each calculation step. Different predefined grid motions can be specified, such as free (Lagrange), fixed (Euler), equipotential, equal spacing and others. As an advantage, distortions can be avoided. On the other hand, additional computation steps are necessary to move and to convert the grid. An example of ALE is shown in Figure 3. Two objects consisting of different materials represented by the colors blue and green before (left side) and after impact (right side). The blue object has an initial velocity in the direction of the green object. The right side of the figure shows the discretization dependent deformation after the impact with the ALE solver. In comparison to the pure Lagrange method (see Figure 1), no lattice distortions occur here.

4) SPH

Smoothed Particle Hydrodynamics is a method which is not based on a fixed topological lattice but on a finite set of particles. These particles are embedded to the material similar to the nodes of the Lagrange method, but their connections are not fixed. However, the particles represent not only mass points, but also interpolation points for the calculation of the physical variables. The calculations are based on the data of the neighboring particles and are scaled by a weighting function. Unlike Lagrange, no grid distortion can occur at SPH, since no grid exists. Related to the Euler method, SPH has the advantage that all material boundaries and interfaces are clearly defined. Figure 4 illustrates two objects consisting of different materials in the SPH frame represented colored particles before (left side) and after impact (right side). The green object has an initial velocity in the direction of the blue object. The right side of the figure shows the discretization dependent deformation after the impact with the SPH solver. As seen in Figure 4. two objects consist of small particles in the SPH frame. Their behavior before and after an impacts differs from the solutions in the Lagrange, Euler or ALE frame.

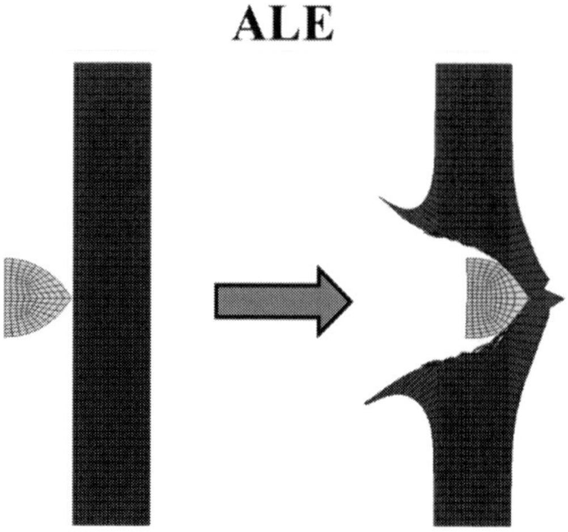

Figure 3. ALE method example.

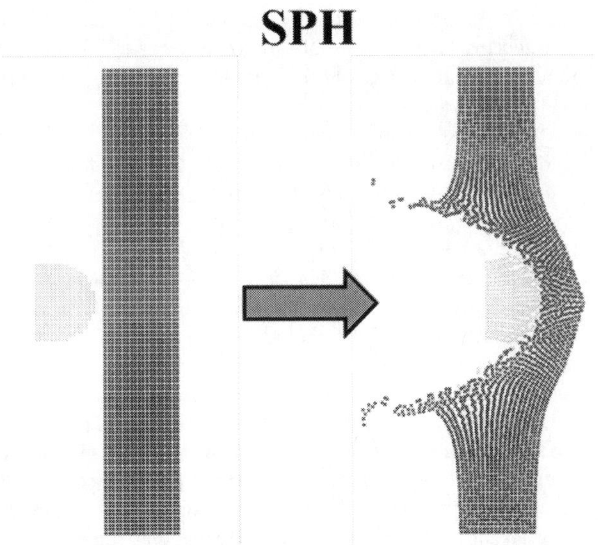

Figure 4. SPH method example.

The SPH method has proven especially useful in the simulation of impact processes on brittle materials [2]. It should be noted that the modelling of the material as particles leads to significantly higher computing effort per time step.

For problems of dynamic fluid-structure interaction and impact, there typically is no single best numerical method which is applicable to all parts of a problem. Techniques to couple types of numerical solvers in a single simulation can allow the use of the most appropriate solver for each domain of the problem.

One of the more important issues, which have to be carefully considered is the issue of mesh size. Different results are obtained if the number of cells per unit length is not adequate. For example, it was found that for penetration studies with eroding long rods, the number of cells on the rod's radius should be at least eleven. The same density of cells should be kept in the target, at least for several projectile radii around its symmetry axis. In order to save computing time, the cell size at farther zones can be gradually increased according to their distance from the symmetry axis. The mesh cell size depends on the specific problem. As an example, a small cell size should be considered in cases where there is a fracture in the projectile or target. It is recommended that while preparing the code for its final runs, the numerical convergence with respect to mesh cell size should be checked. Another important issue, especially when material elements are expected to deform considerably, is the issue of erosion with Lagrangian codes. At large deformations the code may run into trouble when treating heavily deformed elements. The use of the erosion threshold condition is then necessary in order to eliminate elements at a predetermined value of the plastic or geometric deformation. The erosion should be monitored constantly, and when it is too high one should replace the Lagrangian with an Eulerian code.

The goal of this paper is to evaluate an interface between different hydrocodes, computational tools for modeling the behavior of continuous media. In its purest sense, a hydrocode is a computer code for modeling fluid flow at all speeds. For that reason, a structure will be split into a number of small elements. The elements are connected through their nodes (see Figure 5). The mesh divides the object into small elements connected by its nodes.

The behavior (deflection) of the simple elements is well-known and may be calculated and analyzed using simple equations called shape functions. By applying coupling conditions between the elements at their nodes, the overall stiffness of the structure may be built up and the deflection/distortion of any node – and subsequently of the whole structure – can be calculated approximately [12]. Therefore, several runs are necessary: From modeling to calculation to the evaluation and subsequent improvement of the model.

Hydrocodes, or wave propagation codes, are a valuable adjunct to the study of the behavior of metals subjected to high-velocity impact or intense impulsive loading. The combined use of computations, experiments and high-strain-rate material characterization has, in many cases, supplemented the data achievable by experiments alone at considerable savings in both cost and engineering man-hours.

A large database exists of high-pressure Equation-Of-State (EOS) data. Considerable data on high rate deviatoric behavior exists as well although, unlike EOS data, it is not collected in a few compilations but scattered throughout a diverse literature. Experimental techniques exist for determining either EOS or strength data for materials not yet characterized under high-rate loading conditions.

By contrast, computations with non-metallic materials such as composites, concrete, rock, soil and a variety of geological materials are, in effect, research tasks. This is due to several reasons: lack of definitive computational models for high strain rate–temperature–pressure response; lack of a database for EOS and high rate strength data for such materials; lack of test methodologies for anisotropic materials subjected to high-rate loading.

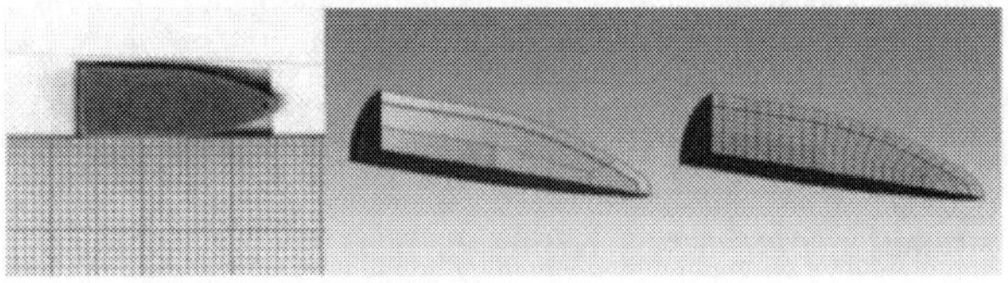

Figure 5. Example grid of a typical bullet.

A large number of ad hoc models exist for explosives, geological materials, concrete and other non-metallics. Many of these lack a firm theoretical foundation. This is an area where considerable research is required, both to devise appropriate test techniques to measure material response under high strain rates, elevated temperatures and high pressures as well as to develop appropriate constitutive models.

B. Interface

In general, an interface connects systems that have different properties with the purpose of exchanging information. For computers, this is mainly the case between software, hardware, peripheral devices and humans. Communication at the interface can be either in one direction, such as a remote control or keyboard, or in both directions, such as a touch screen or a network adapter [13].

In the context of numerical simulation of blast and impact processes, an interface is necessary to ensure an effective coupling of CFD / FEM simulations between the software Abaqus and ANSYS. For our research, ANSYS is to be used to provide data from simulated explosions using Euler-Lagrange coupling. On the other hand, the structure, which is affected by the blasting is simulated by Abaqus. The developed Interface has the task of conveying the data between ANSYS and Abaqus, so that the individual simulation steps can be performed successively with respect to the successive transfer of data.

V. Experimental Section

In computing, an interface is a shared boundary across two separate components of a computer system exchange information. The exchange can be between software, computer hardware, peripheral devices, humans and combinations of these. Some computer hardware devices such as a touchscreen can both send and receive data through the interface, while others such as a mouse, microphone or joystick operate one way only [13].

Coupled FEA/CFD analysis is an alternative technique, where separate FEA and CFD codes are used for solid and fluid regions, respectively, with a smooth exchange of information between the two codes to ensure continuity of blast loading data. The main merit of the approach is to enable users to take full advantages of both CFD and FEA capabilities.

The objective of this work is to develop an interface between ANSYS Autodyn and Abaqus. The software ANSYS is used to solve linear and non-linear problems of structural mechanics, computational fluid dynamics, acoustics and various other engineering sciences [14]. Here, ANSYS will provide data from the simulation of blast effects. The capability to couple Eulerian and Lagrangian frames in ANSYS is helpful in blast field modeling. The Eulerian frame is best suited for representing explosive detonations, because the material flows through a geometrically constant grid that can easily handle the large deformations associated with gas and fluid flow. The structure is modeled with the Lagrangian frame in Abaqus. Abaqus supports familiar interactive computer-aided engineering concepts such as feature-based, parametric modeling, interactive and scripted operation, and GUI customization [15].

First, every possibility of transferring the data from ANSYS outputs to Abaqus inputs has to be detected. A summary of this process is shown in Figure 6.

ANSYS will provide the data by generating a data set for the blast loading. This data set will include snapshots of given points in time. At this stage there is a data set of five points in time, between 0.0291s and 0.0475s (after detonation). Related to the points in time this data set includes the pressure values with Cartesian coordinates based on the simulation of the spread of explosive materials (see Figure 7). A script is coded to read the blast loading data in Abaqus. This script, coded in Python, uses the line interface in Abaqus directly. Python is an interpreted high-level programming language for general-purpose programming. It provides constructs that enable clear programming on both small and large scales.

First, a blast loading data is generated in ANSYS and saved as a normal text file in .txt format. The data set will be split to separate the different types of information. After that, a list will be created to save the data and connect the related time points to the coordinates and pressure values. At this point, there is a possibility to use linear interpolation between the five time points to generate a larger data base. After reading and saving the data set, the script will load the model used for impact tests in Abaqus. A surface of the model must be selected to project the blast data on it.

The goal is to investigate the impact of the blast data on a full vehicle model in Abaqus. This work starts with a less complex model to validate the function of the script and the interface itself. The first model was a basic rectangle to be strained by the pressure data. Afterwards, two more complex models were tested successfully. This approach will lead to a surface similar to the silhouette of high security vehicles (see Figure 8).

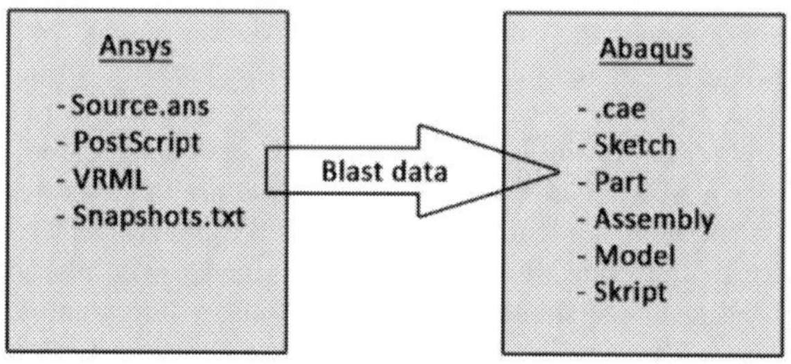

Figure 6. Inputs and outputs for an interface between Ansys and Abaqus.

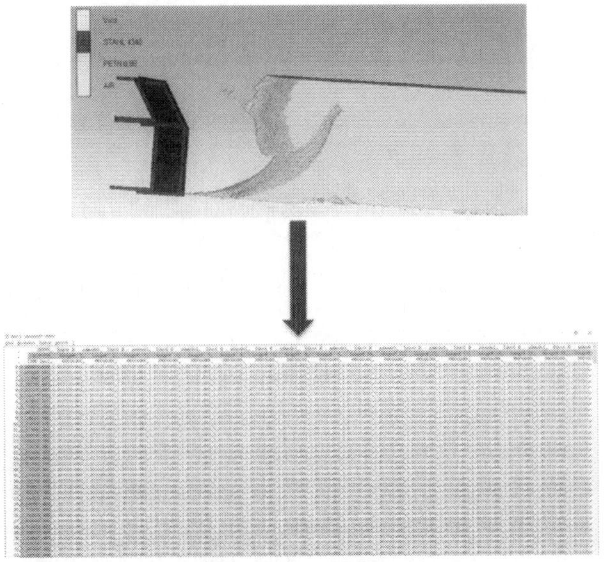

Figure 7. Transferring pressure date from a blast simulation into a a common text file.

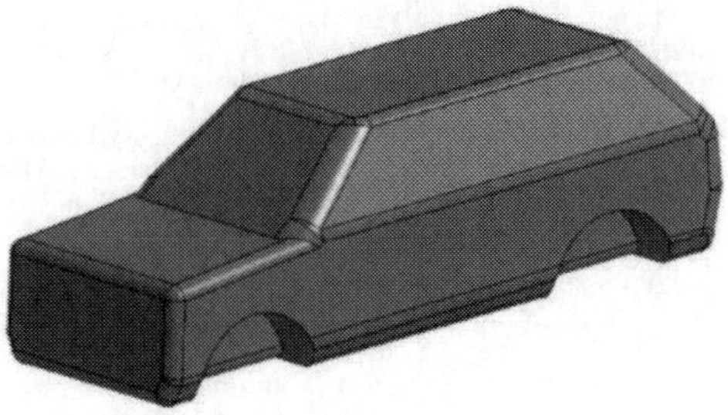

Figure 8. Testing structure in Abaqus with the coarse appearance of a vehicle.

The coupling is realized through an iterative loop between the FEA and CFD simulations, with communications ensuring continuity of shock compression data across the coupled boundaries between the FEA and CFD models. In the coupling process, intermediate individual FEA and CFD solutions are obtained in turn with dynamically updated boundary conditions.

To avoid exceptional deadlock of the individual CFD simulations, appropriate maximum numbers of iterations are assigned for each CFD model.

Testing means that the spatially discretized model is loaded with pressure. The change over time is decisive. An example is shown in Figure 9. . The unarmored SUV model was loaded with a typical explosive charge. The load on the vehicle is made visible by color coding from low strain (blue) to very high strain (red). The deformation on the sheet metal body parts is clearly shown. This data can be used to simply analyze vulnerabilities. The goal is, however, to use complete vehicle models and to carry out realistic investigations.

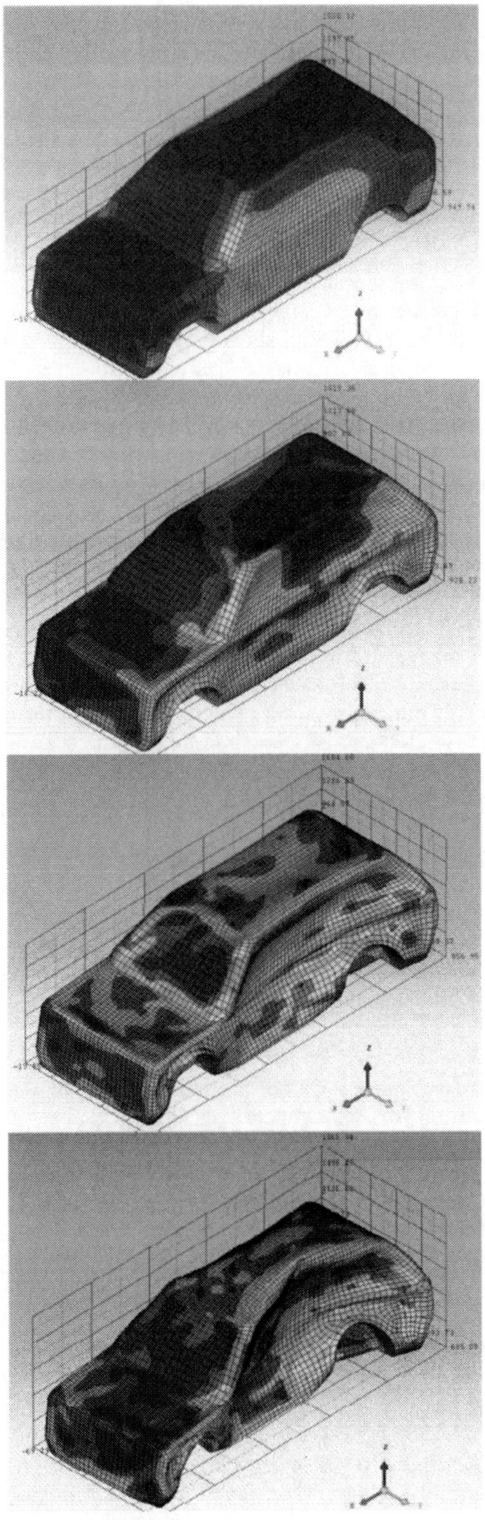

Figure 9. Simulated test structure (unarmed SUV) and deformation process after 3, 5, 10 and 20 ms (images arranged from top to bottom in order of increasing time).

VI. Outlook

There are a variety of approaches in implementing the coupled FEA/CFD analysis. One is generally called "strong coupling," where data have to be transferred between ANSYS Autodyn and ABAQUS in every single time step. A "semistrong coupling" can get along with a smaller set of date, using mathematical interpolation for a sufficient approximation. The third concept is a "weak coupling" solution. Here, neural networks and deep learning can be used to replicate blast effects on different vehicle structures. These approaches are going to be tested in a next step.

Furthermore, a larger blast loading data set has to be created in ANSYS. This will allow a more accurate illustration of blast effects on vehicle structures. Smaller time steps will enable a linear interpolation with a higher accuracy. Different explosives are going to be tested to expand the data base. The next step will be a model for the reflection of blast waves and dynamic changes of pressure values. Using a full vehicle model will provide important information about the behavior of armored structures under blast effects. But to validate the results of the simulation, more ballistic trials are needed. Based on the difficulties of full vehicle model simulations, the implementation of an automatic surface detection has to be taken into consideration. This could be helpful if a large number of different vehicles are investigated. In order to create a user-friendly interface, it is possible to generate the script as a plug-in which can be started from the Abaqus user surface directly.

By using pre-defined blast data to create forces as vectors on our vehicle structures, the proposal can be generalized. Then, FEA analysis can be done with other software suites as well. Right now, the concept is not applicable to other systems. This is a major disadvantage and part of our future work. Furthermore, a parallelization of the problem should be considered.

VII. Conclusion and Future Work

A technique for efficiently coupling FEA/CFD for the simulation of blast effects is described. An interface between ANSYS and Abaqus was created to provide blast data sets. The data sets from ANSYS include snapshots from the blast simulation saved at different points in time. The interface is coded in Python and also contains the possibility to use linear interpolation on the data sets.

A good agreement of blast load test data and simulation results was observed. Furthermore, it is shown that the coupled solutions can be obtained in sufficiently short turn-around times for use in design. These solutions can be used as the basis of an iterative optimization process. They are a valuable adjunct to the study of the behavior of vehicle structures subjected to high-velocity impact or intense impulsive loading. The combined use of computations, experiments and high-strain-rate material characterization has, in many cases, supplemented the data achievable by experiments alone at considerable savings in both cost and engineering man-hours.

References

[1] E. Hansen, N. Ehlers, A. Ramezani, and H. Rothe, "Developing an Interface between ANSYS and Abaqus to Simulate Blast Effects on High Security Vehicles," The Eighth International Conference on Advances in System Simulation (SIMUL 2016) IARIA, Aug. 2016, pp. 73-76, ISBN 978-1-61208-442-8.

[2] A. Ramezani and H. Rothe, "Investigation of Solver Technologies for the Simulation of Brittle Materials," The Sixth International Conference on Advances in System Simulation (SIMUL 2014) IARIA, pp. 236-242, Oct. 2014, ISBN 978-61208-371-1.

[3] J. Zukas, "Introduction to Hydrocodes". Elsevier Science, 2004.

[4] A. M. S. Hamouda and M. S. J. Hashmi, "Modelling the impact and penetration events of modern engineering materials: Characteristics of computer codes and material models," Journal of Materials Processing Technology, vol. 56, pp. 847-862, Jan. 1996.

[5] D. J. Benson, "Computational methods in Lagrangian and Eulerian hydrocodes," Computer Methods in Applied Mechanics and Engineering, vol. 99, pp. 235-394, Sep. 1992, doi: 10.1016/0045-7825(92)90042-I.

[6] M. Oevermann, S. Gerber, and F. Behrendt, "Euler-Lagrange/DEM simulation of wood gasification in a bubbling fluidized bed reactor," Particuology, vol. 7, pp. 307-316, Aug. 2009, doi: 10.1016/j.partic.2009.04.004.

[7] D. L. Hicks and L. M. Liebrock, "SPH hydrocodes can be stabilized with shape-shifting," Computers & Mathematics with Applications, vol. 38, pp. 1-16, Sep. 1999, doi: 10.1016/S0898-1221(99)00210-2.

[8] X. Quan, N. K. Birnbaum, M. S. Cowler, and B. I. Gerber, "Numerical Simulations of Structural Deformation under Shock and Impact Loads using a Coupled Multi-Solver Approach," 5th Asia-Pacific Conference on Shock and Impact Loads on Structures, Hunan, China, Nov. 2003, pp. 152-161.

[9] N. V. Bermeo, M. G. Mendoza, and A. G. Castro, "Semantic Representation of CAD Models Based on the IGES Standard," Computer Science, vol. 8265, pp. 157-168, Dec. 2001, doi: 10.1007/ 978-3-642-45114-013.

[10] J. Sarkar, "Computer Aided Design: A Conceptual Approach," CRC Press, December 2014.

[11] C. E. Anderson, "An overview of the theory of hydrocodes," International journal of impact engineering, 5.1-4, pp 33-59, 1987.

[12] G.-S. Collins, "An Introduction to Hydrocode Modeling," Applied Modelling and Computation Group, Imperial College London, 2002.

[13] IEEE 100 – "The Authoritative Dictionary Of IEEE Standards Terms," NYC, NY, USA: IEEE Press, 2000, pp. 574-575, ISBN 0-7381-2601-2.

[14] ANSYS. CAE. *Structures: FEA Simulation*. [Online]. Available from: http://www.ansys.com [retrieved: June, 2018].

[15] Abaqus *Complete Solutions for Realistic Simulation*. [Online]. Available from: http://www.3ds.com/products-services/simulia/products/abaqus/abaquscae/ [retrieved: June, 2018]

Generation of a Geodetic Line on Any Given Surface

Anna von Pestalozza, Stefan Weichert, Arash Ramezani, Hendrik Rothe
Chair of Short-Time Dynamics
University of the Federal Armed Forces
Hamburg, Germany
Email: pestalozza@hsu-hh.de, s-weichert@web.de, ramezani@hsu-hh.de, rothe@hsu-hh.de

Abstract—**The calculation of geodetic lines plays an important role in many applications, such as the minimisation of material in manufacturing processes. Many manufacturing steps, such as cutting or attaching layers on curved surfaces, suffer from loss of material. In order to minimise wastage of material, geodetic lines can be employed to find a cutting pattern for the given material with minimal distortion. This paper presents an automatable algorithm that numerically calculates geodetic lines on any given surface. The result is evaluated with a practical example by comparing the numerical result and the analytical solution.**

Keywords-Geodetic Line; Surface Analysis; Materials Technology.

I. INTRODUCTION

This paper is based on the assumptions that the material of the given surface is of finite thickness and of low elasticity which leads to the necessity of minimising loss of material. Furthermore, the starting point of the presented research is the approach given in [1] for finding geodetic l ines between two points. The main idea is to successively calculate distances from the starting point which is improved by the fast marching method. In the following, an algorithm for extracting the geodetic line as well as for further improving it is derived.

For cutting a curved surface either sectional planes or geodetic lines can be used. The graphical approximation of flattened material stripes of an originally curved surface having been cut by the procedures of applying sectional planes and calculating geodetic lines clearly show that the cutting with the geodetic lines provides straight edges when flattened whereas the sectional planes result in curved edges which leads to a higher amount of material loss. However, sectional planes are much easier to apply and less time consuming than the analytical calculation of geodetic lines which is not even possible in many cases. Thus, this paper aims to provide an algorithm which approximates analytical geodetic lines on any given surface.

The paper is divided in five sections. After the Introduction, the calculation of the shortest distance on a triangulated mesh is shown in Section II followed by Section III about the extraction of the geodetic line. In Section IV a straightening algorithm for improvement of the geodetic line is presented. The paper ends with a concluding paragraph in Section V and an outlook to future work on this project.

II. CALCULATION OF SHORTEST DISTANCES ON A TRIANGULATED MESH

In this paper, the procedure of the Fast Marching Method (FMM) is used [3] for calculating the shortest distances on a triangulated mesh. Basically, this method approximates the distances of all points surrounding the starting point successively by a wave front until it reaches the given ending point. For the following procedure it is assumed that starting and ending point of the geodetic line which is to be approximated are given.

A. Procedure

In the FMM, the vertices of all triangles in the mesh are divided into several groups which are sets of vertices.

1) Fixed vertex set (FVS): contains initially only the starting points; vertices which are points of the shortest distance are added in the procedure.

2) Close vertex set (CVS): contains initially no vertices; vertices which are close to the point that is investigated in the current iteration of the loop are added.

3) Fixed vertex set (FVS): contains all vertices of the mesh that are not contained in FVS.

Two situations can be distinguished: Only one starting point is given and more than one starting point is given. If there is only one starting point, the distances T_i of its direct neighbours have to be calculated and the neighbours are added to the CVS. If there is more than one starting point, the points a_0, a_1, and a_2 which are part of a triangle of the mesh containing exactly two points in FVS have to be determined. After computing their distances T_0, T_1, and T_2 to the starting value, the points a_0, a_1, and a_2 are added to CVS. After these initial steps, the following loop starts:

- The point a_i, i = 0, 1, 2 with the shortest distance T_i to the starting value is moved to FVS and is now the point of origin for further investigations. This point is called trial.
- The distances T_i of all points in UVS∪CVS which are adjacent to triangles containing trial and a point in FVS are computed and moved to CVS.

In each iteration, one point is added to FVS and its neighbours are added to CVS. The algorithm terminates when FVS contains every vertex which is part of a line resulting in the shortest distance from starting to ending point.

B. Calculation of Distance T

For calculating the distance T the method presented in [3] is used. It requires that one point, P_1, of known distance T_1 is the origin and that another point, P_2, of known distance T_2 is on the x-axis.

1) Procedure: The distance T_3 of the third point P_3 is calculated in terms of T_1, T_2 and the connecting vectors v_i with $v_i = P_i - P_1$, in particular $(v_3)_x$ and $(v_3)_y$, i.e., the projections of v_3 onto the new basis vectors, which are calculated as follows: To change the default, adjust the template as follows:

a) One point is set as the origin (P_1):

$$v_i = P_i - P_1$$

b) The coordinate system is transformed where:

$$e_x = \frac{(p_2 - p_1)}{|p_2 - p_1|} = \frac{(v_2)}{|v_2|}$$

$$e_y = \frac{(v_3 - e_x \cdot (e_x \cdot v_3))}{|(v_3 - e_x \cdot (e_x \cdot v_3)|} = \frac{(v_3 \cdot |v_2|^2 - v_2 \cdot (v_2 \cdot v_3))}{|(v_3 \cdot |v_2|^2 - v_2 \cdot (v_2 \cdot v_3)|}$$

c) The distance of v_3 to the new coordinate system is computed where O_x is the x-coordinate at which the origin of the new coordinate is located and O_y is the relative y-coordinate:

$$O_x = \frac{1}{2}\frac{(v_2)_x^2 + T_1^2 - T_2^2}{(v_2)_x}$$

$$O_y = \pm\sqrt{T_1^2 - \frac{((v_2)_x^2 + T_1^2 - T_2^2)^2}{4(v_2)_x^2}} = \pm\sqrt{T_1^2 - O_x^2}$$

$$T_3 = O_x \cdot e_x + O_y \cdot e_y - v_3$$

A challenge with this method is that there are always two possible virtual origins due to $\pm O_y$. In [3] it is stated that this is solved by calculating both distances and taking the larger value. However, there are situations where the smaller value is the correct one. This happens, presumably, mostly or only when P_3 is not in front of the wavefront but beside. Such a situation occurs when the distance of a point in the CVS is recalculated. To mitigate this issue in a simple way, the recalculated value for the distance T is only stored if it is smaller than the existing one.

2) Accuracy: The algorithm was tested on a sphere with equally spaced points as shown in Figure 1. The starting point, i.e., the point with distance $T = 0$ is chosen to be the north pole. The points are numerated such that one whole circle at constant θ is taken. Thus, plotting the distance over the index results in plateaus of constant distance (see Figure 1 b and c).

III. Extracting the Geodetic Line

In the second section, the shortest distance from starting to ending point on the triangulated mesh is determined. In order to approximate the geodetic line, a line of shortest distance can be backtracked along the points in FVS. The real geodetic line, however, does not necessarily consist only of vertices but of points on edges of the triangles as well. In the following the first approximation of the geodetic line is denoted by Γ_0.

A. Method of Minimum Distance

The Method of Minimum Distance approximates Γ_0 with regard to the calculated distances T. It iterates the following procedure and can be modified through two different options:

1. The neighbor N of the previous point is determined which fulfills one of the following requirements:

a) Option 1: N has the lowest distance T_N of all provided neighbours.

b) Option 2: N is the point of neighbours for which the value of the distance T_N added to the distance from the previous point p is minimal

2. The resulting neighbor N is appended to Γ_0.

This method extracts the geodetic line very quickly but does not provide a good approximation, neither with Option 1 nor Option 2, especially when the grid is very uniform. Also, the points of the geodetic line are still only located on vertices. Therefore, the *gradient method* was implemented.

B. The Gradient Method

The gradient method provides an approach to extract the geodetic line dissociated from the vertices. To determine the direction in which the geodetic line propagates the gradient of the distance T, approximated with the three distances for each point in each triangle, is used.

1) Approximation of the gradient in a triangle:

The gradient in a triangle with vertices i, j and k is given by

$$(\vec{\nabla}T)_{(i,j,k)} = -\frac{\vec{n}}{|n|^2} \times \left(T_i\vec{e}_{jk} + T_j\vec{e}_{ki} + T_k\vec{e}_{ij}\right),$$

where

$$\vec{e}_{a,b} = \vec{x}_b - \vec{x}_a$$

are the vectors connecting the vertices a and b and $\vec{n}$ is the surface normal of the triangle:

$$\vec{n} = \vec{e}_{ki} \times \vec{e}_{jk}$$

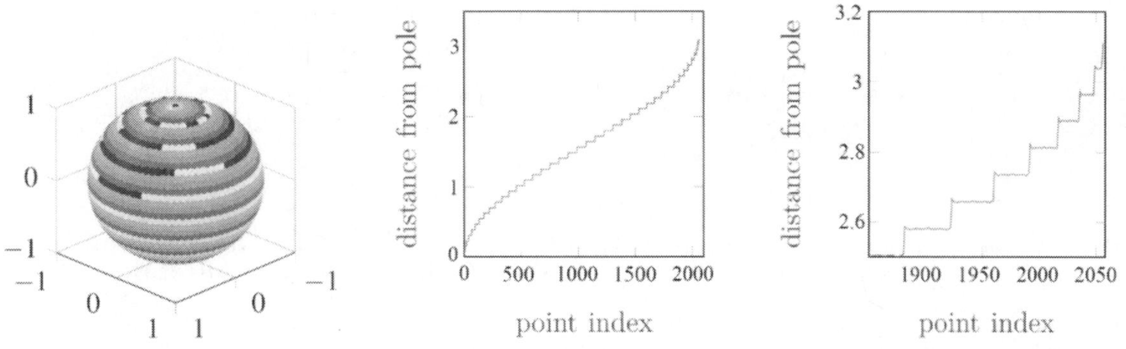

(a) The colourmap was chosen to be repeating 10 times so that intra-ring fluctuations are visible.

(b) Staircase-distances emerging from the ring-after-ring data-structure

(c) Zoom of the upper "stairs" shows oscillations (visible in intra-ring colour changes in (A).)

Figure 1. Distances on homogeneously sampled sphere. The index starts at the south pole and increases ring by ring until the north pole is reached. Distances are calculated from the south pole via the fast marching method.

Note that the connecting vectors $\vec{e}_{ij}$, $\vec{e}_{jk}$ and $\vec{e}_{ki}$ are circular, i.e., that

$$\vec{e}_{ij} + \vec{e}_{jk} + \vec{e}_{ki} = 0$$

In Figure 2, a sketch of a triangle with its gradient is shown for an example set of distance values T_i, T_j, T_k.

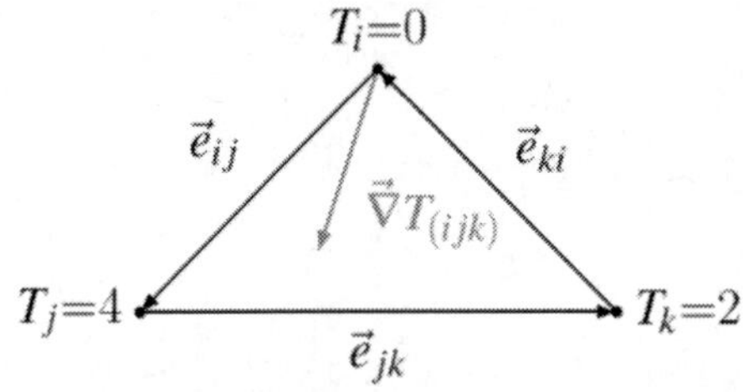

Figure 2. Three points (i, j, k) of a triangle with distance values T and the approximated gradient $(\vec{\nabla}T)_{(i,j,k)}$

2) Extracting the Geodetic Line with the Gradient Method:

The basic concept of the gradient method is to generate a line g for each triangle from the previous point p of the geodetic line and the gradient of T

$$g : \vec{x}(\lambda) = \vec{p} + \lambda\vec{\nabla}T_{(ijk)}$$

and to find its point of intersection with the edges of adjacent triangles. For the choice of edges to intersect g with, one has to consider whether the previous point p is on a vertex or an edge. If p is on a vertex, the following procedure is applied:

1. The negative gradients of the adjacent triangles are computed.
2. A triangle determined whose negative gradient points into the triangle itself.
3. The line g is intersected with the edge of that triangle on the opposite side.
4. The point of intersection is added to Γ_0.

If no triangle is found whose negative gradient points into the triangle itself, the neighbour N with the smallest distance T to the previous point p is added to Γ_0.

If p lies on an edge, a different procedure is used:

1. The triangle which is adjacent to p and was not used for the prior calculation of p itself has to be identified.
2. The line g is intersected with the two remaining edges, if the negative gradient points into the triangle.

If the negative gradient does not point into the triangle, the previous p is moved to the vertex of the same edge that has the smaller distance T.

Special case: It might happen that p lies on a boundary edge. This case can be resolved by moving p to the vertex of the same triangle with a smaller distance T. If p lies on a boundary vertex, the above-mentioned procedure can be applied without further arrangements. As already mentioned, this is a special case. Therefore, this will not be considered in the further course.

3) Performance of the Gradient Method

The algorithm approximates the real geodetic line in many test cases very precisely in accurate time. In case that real geodetic line runs near or along a line of edges without passing through several triangles or without changing the lane over the course of many points, the calculated geodetic line tends to stick to one lane and very late moves over to the other. This cannot be taken care of by the improvement algorithm which is described in the next section unless it is run for a lot more iterations than usual which is expensive. However, this special case is not problematic unless one

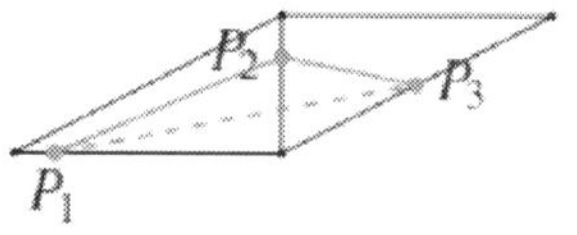

(a) $P_{i,j}$ lies on an edge

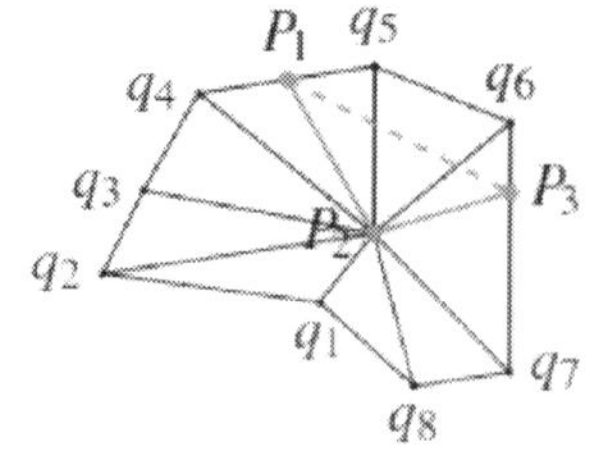

(b) $P_{i,j}$ lies on a vertex.

Figure 3. The two cases of a point of the geodesic Γ_i needing correction. For readability, $P_{i-1,j}$, $P_{i,j}$ and $P_{i+1,j}$ have been replaced by P_1, P_2 and P_3, respectively. The dashed line denotes the corrected path.

wants to find the real geodetic line with even higher accuracy than already provided. For this, one could calculate the geodetic line and refine the triangulation around it to redo the whole calculation with the new triangulation until it converges.

IV. Improving the Approximation of the Geodetic Line

In the previous section we have generated an initial approximation Γ_0 for the geodetic line between two points on a triangulated mesh in three-dimensional space. As this is just a first approximation, an algorithm for improving Γ_0 is required. The improvement can be achieved by moving the points on vertices of the geodetic line along the edges of the mesh to shorten the length of Γ_0.

A. *Criterion for Improvement of the Geodetic Line*

According to [2] the shortest path is given by the straightest path for triangulated surfaces. 'Straight' is defined as follows: After taking all triangles that the approximation Γ_{i-1} passes through and unfolding them into a plane, the path Γ_i is the shortest when it is a straight line in the planar view. Therefore, the algorithm for improvement aims at straightening the path in the unfolded planar view.

B. *The straightening algorithm*

For this section the *i*-th version of the path is denoted as Γ_i and $P_{i,j}$ the *j*-th point of the *i*-th path. For the following let $P_{i,j}$ be the point to be corrected using the information about $P_{i,j+1}$ and $P_{i,j-1}$. The idea is to locally straighten the path by moving the central point of the three, i.e., $P_{i,j}$. To ensure that the geodetic line converges and actually becomes shorter with each iteration, the updated $P_{i+1,j}$ for the updated path Γ_{i+1} is calculated using the points which have already been updated during this iteration, i.e., $P_{i+1,j-1}$ instead of $P_{i,j-1}$. For readability, we omit the "+1" in $P_{i+1,j-1}$, but take care of it by only keeping one Γ stored and updating it with each step during each iteration.

There are always two cases to be considered: $P_{i,j}$ lies on an edge or on a vertex as can be seen in Figure 3.

1) *$P_{i,j}$ lies on an edge:*

If $P_{i,j}$ lies on an edge, the two triangles adjacent to $P_{i,j}$ are unfolded. The point of intersection of the connecting line between $P_{i,j+1}$ and $P_{i,j-1}$ and the edge that $P_{i,j}$ lies on are calculated. If the point of intersection does not lie between the two vertices of the edge, the closer vertex is chosen to be the corrected point instead in this case.

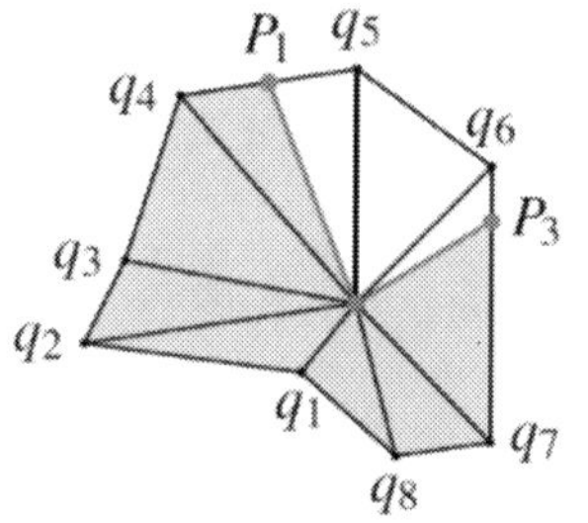

(a) Angle θ_r

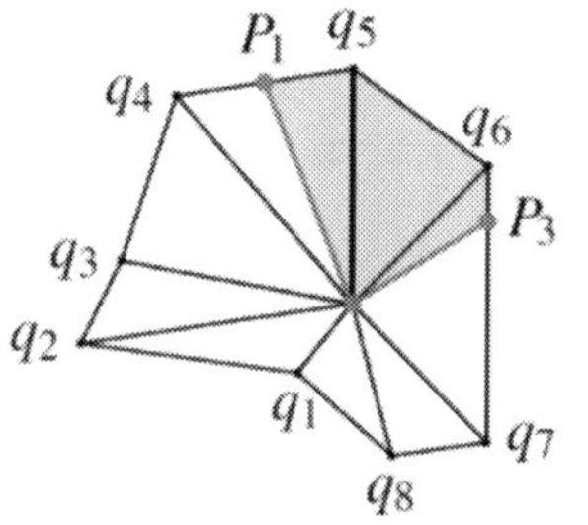

(b) Angle θ_l

Figure 4. Notation of angles in the star-like structure of S_k

2) *$P_{i,j}$ lies on a vertex*

If the point that is to be corrected coincides with a vertex, the procedure becomes more complicated. Let S_k be the set of triangles that have $P_{i,j}$ as the central vertex, then several cases can be distinguished. Firstly, there are two simple cases which can be easily taken care of numerically:

a) If all three points ($P_{i,-1,j}$, $P_{i,j}$ and $P_{i,+1,j}$) are part of the same triangle, $P_{i,j}$ is removed from Γ.

b) If $P_{i,j+1}$ *or* $P_{i,j-1}$ lies on an edge that is not part of the boundary of S_k, it is removed from Γ.

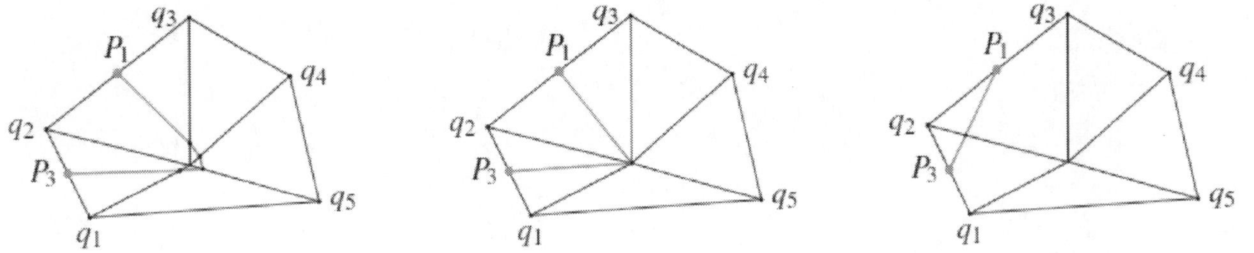

(a) The path is stuck at a vertex

(b) After ten iterations all points close to a vertex are removed and replaced by one point which is directly located on the vertex.

(c) The next iteration corrects this point and the detour is removed.

Figure 5. Correction of points surrounding a vertex

For all other cases ($P_{i,\,j+1}$ and $P_{i,j-1}$ belong to two different triangles) the vertices around $P_{i,j}$ are sorted and the left and right hand angles, θ_l and θ_r, are calculated in order to characterize the vertex as can be seen in Figure 4. These angles are given by the sum of the central angles of the triangles which are obtained by splitting the star-like structure of S_k along the path $P_{i,-1,j} \rightarrow P_{i,j} \rightarrow P_{i,+1,j}$.

Three main cases can be distinguished:

a) $\theta = 2\pi$: euclidean

b) $\theta = \theta_l + \theta_r > 2\pi$: hyperbolic

c) $\theta < 2\pi$: spherical

These three cases are taken care of differently where θ is defined as left or right hand angle.

a) Euclidean: S_k can be unfolded isometrically. After unfolding, $P_{i,\,j+1}$ or $P_{i,j-1}$ are joined in the unfolded S_k and the intersections with the edges added to Γ.

b) Hyperbolic:

a. If θ_l and θ_r are greater than π: no correction is needed.

b. If θ_l and θ_r are smaller than π, that side of S_k is unfolded and $P_{i,\,j+1}$ as well as $P_{i,j-1}$ are joined in the same manner as in the Euclidean case.

c) Spherical: The part of S_k with smaller $\theta_{l/r}$ is unfolded and $P_{i,\,j+1}$ or $P_{i,j-1}$ are joined as in the Euclidean case.

In all three cases the part of S_k with smaller $\theta_{l/r}$ has to be unfolded and the points of intersection have to be calculated.

In test runs, it was observed that points which are very close to vertices keep approaching the vertex which they are close to without coinciding and adopting its value. Therefore, every 10 iterations the path is scanned for points on Γ for which this might be the case. These points are moved to the vertex instead. All following points that approach the same vertex are deleted from the path. This is necessary because otherwise curves in the path will never pass over a vertex. The effect of the scanning of the path and the movement of points to vertices is shown in Figure 5.

V. Exemplary Results

To test the capability of the gradient method and the straightening algorithm a geometry was chosen for which exact geodetic lines can be analytically computed for reference.

A plane with a half cylinder barrier is generated and the geodetic line between two points on either side of the half cylinder is calculated, first analytically, then using the presented algorithm as shown in Figure 6.

In Figure 6, several aspects can be seen: Beginning at the ending point (on the right-hand side of the half cylinder) the distances of the other points are calculated by the FMM. These increase up to the starting point (on the left-hand side of the half cylinder). For clarity, the colour palette was chosen such that it is repeated five times. The black line shows the analytically calculated geodetic line. The red crosses show the points of the geodetic line which was calculated with the above-described algorithm.

In the left image the calculation is stopped after the extraction using the gradient method. For the right image the extracted geodetic line was improved by using the technique described in Subsection IV-B.

As can be seen, the straightening algorithm removed a few deviations visible close to the upper right end of the geodetic line. The straightening algorithm ran 50 times but most of the improvement was already achieved after 5 iterations.

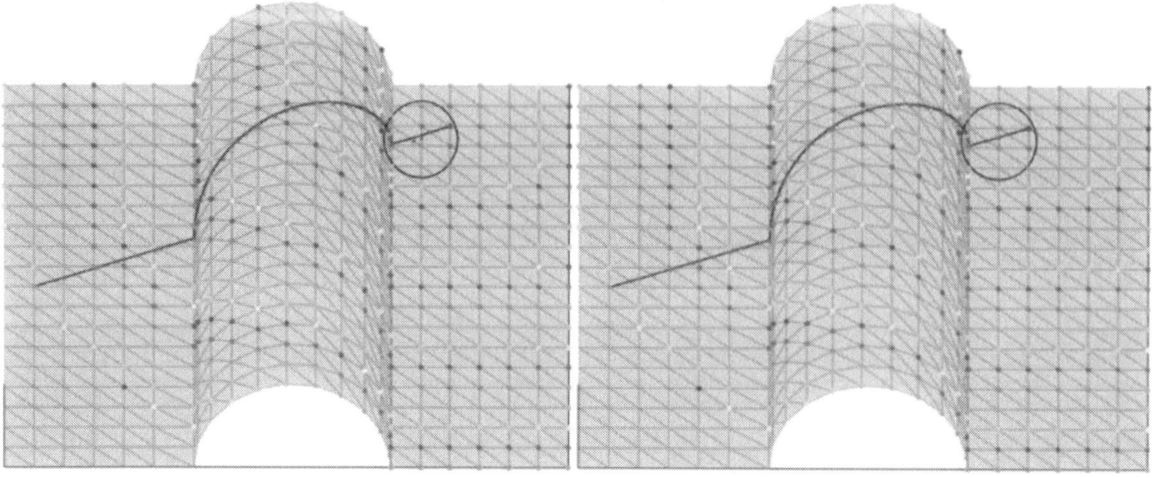

Figure 6. Result of fast marching method (both), geodesic extraction (left) and improvement algorithm (right).

VI. Conclusion and Future Work

An algorithm for calculating a geodetic line on a given surface and a technique for its further improvement are described. The goal was to derive an accurate numerically determined geodetic line. Further steps could feature an extension of the algorithm, such that several geodetic lines on one surface can be found by iterating over the algorithm. To further improve, analyse and straighten the geodetic line, the unfolding of surfaces with the least distortion could be investigated and automatised. Moreover, the change in accuracy dependent of the number of elements in the triangulated mesh could be investigated in order to define and optimize the relation between these two quantities.

References

[1] J. M. F. Linhard, Numeric-Mechanical Investigation of the Planning Process of Membrane Structures, PhD thesis, Technische Universität München, 2009.

[2] D. Martínez, L. Velho, and P. C. Carvalho, Computing geodesics on triangular meshes, Computers & Graphics 29(5):667 – 675, 2005.

[3] M. Novotni und R. Klein, Computing geodesic distances on triangular meshes, Journal of WDCG, 10(1-2):341-347, 2002.